Chicken

BLOOMSBURY KITCHEN LIBRARY

Chicken

Bloomsbury Books
London

This edition published 1994 by Bloomsbury Books,
an imprint of The Godfrey Cave Group,
42 Bloomsbury Street, London, WC1B 3QJ.

ISBN 1 85471 542 9

Printed and bound in Great Britain.

Contents

Stir-Fried Chopped Chicken on Lettuce Leaves 7
Sautéed Chicken Breasts with Liver and Grapes 8
Chicken Cutlets with Herbs and Tomato Sauce 9
Chicken Breasts Sautéed with Coriander 10
Sautéed Chicken Breasts with Raspberry Sauce 11
Chicken with Mustard, Caraway Seeds and Chervil 12
Chicken Riesling 13
Chicken, Aubergine and Tomato Sauté 14
Chicken Paprika with Yogurt 15
Chicken Breasts with Tarragon and Tomato 16
Chicken with Broccoli, Red Onions and Cashew Nuts 17
Chicken Breasts with Apricots, Bourbon and Pecans 18
Stir-Fried Chicken with Red Cabbage and Chilies 19
Poached Chicken with Fennel 20
Poached Chicken Strips in Gingered Orange Sauce 21
Red Pepper and Chicken Spirals 22
Poached Chicken with Black Bean Onion Sauce 23
Cranberried Chicken 24
Chicken Poached in Milk and Curry 25
Chicken Fan with Basil-Tomato Sauce 26
Chicken Legs with Celery, Shallots and Red Onion 27
Spanish-Style Chicken and Saffron Rice 28
Orange-Glazed Chicken 29
Saffron Chicken Stew 30
Braised Chicken with Plums and Lemons 31
Chicken with Orange and Onion 32
Braised Chicken with Red and Green Apples 33
Chicken Braised with Haricot Beans and Tomatoes 34
Jellied Chicken with Lemon and Dill 35
Chicken Mole 36
Curried Chicken with Chutney and Raisins 37
Chicken with Dark Rum, Papaya, Mango and Banana 38

Chicken Drumsticks Cacciatore 39
Chicken Legs Stewed with Prunes 40
Lemon-Mustard Chicken with Root Vegetables 41
Braised Chicken, Almonds and Chick-Peas 42
Chicken Casserole with Dried Fruits and Onions 43
Chicken Fricassee with Watercress... 44
Braised Chicken with Potatoes, Leeks and Kale 45
Chicken Rolled in Vine Leaves 46
Plum-Coated Chicken with Chinese Cabbage 47
Honey-Basil Chicken 48
Baked Chicken Breasts Stuffed with Tahini 49
Baked Chicken Legs Stuffed with Millet 50
Chicken Pillows 51
Spicy Yogurt-Baked Chicken Thighs 52
Spinach-Stuffed Chicken Breasts 53
Cajun Chicken Wings 54
Chicken Wrapped in Crisp Phyllo 55
Chicken with Peanuts and Ginger Sauce 56
Yogurt-Baked Chicken with Pimientos and Chives 57
Crêpes Filled with Chicken and Sweetcorn 58
Peach-Glazed Poussins with Ginger 59
Oven-Fried Cinnamon Chicken.. 60
Chicken Breasts with Courgettes in Red Wine Sauce 61
Lime and Mint Chicken 62
Grilled Chicken with Malt Vinegar and Basil 63
Chicken Breasts with Radishes 64
Chicken Thighs Grilled with Sherry and Honey 65
Dry Martini Poussins... 66
Thyme-Roasted Chicken 67
Roast Chicken with Apples, Turnips and Garlic........................ 68
Cold Chicken and Asparagus with Lemon-Tarragon 69
Spatchcocked Chicken with Basil-Yogurt Sauce 70
Chilled Chicken Couscous with Lime 71

Stir-Fried Chopped Chicken on Lettuce Leaves

Serves 6

Working
time: about
30 minutes

Total time:
about
45 minutes

Calories
275

Protein
27g

Cholesterol
65mg

Total fat
13g

Saturated fat
2g

Sodium
590mg

0 g	chicken breast, finely chopped	1¼ lb	1 tbsp	finely chopped fresh ginger root	1 tbsp
5 g	dried Chinese mushrooms	½ oz	2	garlic cloves, finely chopped	2
tbsp	cornflour	1 tbsp	2	spring onions, finely chopped	2
tbsp	dry sherry	2 tbsp	90 g	water chestnuts, chopped	3 oz
tsp	salt	¼ tsp	250 g	bamboo shoots, chopped	8 oz
tsp	Sichuan peppercorns	1 tsp	60 g	lean ham, finely chopped	2 oz
	iceberg lettuces	2	3 tbsp	low-sodium soy sauce	3 tbsp
tbsp	safflower oil	3 tbsp	2 tsp	dark sesame oil	2 tsp

ak the mushrooms in a bowl of hot water for
) minutes. Stir, then soak for another 20 minutes
efore draining. Cut off and discard the stems, slice
e mushrooms thinly, and set them aside.

In a bowl, mix the cornflour and the sherry. Add
e salt and the chicken. Combine well and set aside
marinate for at least 15 minutes.

Meanwhile, in a small, heavy frying pan, toss the
eppercorns over medium heat for 3 to 4 minutes.
emove from the pan and crush. Set aside.

Carefully separate the lettuce leaves. Trim to
roduce 12 cup-like leaves.

Heat a wok over high heat. Add 2 tbsps safflower

oil and swirl to coat the pan. Add chicken and stir-
fry until the meat loses its pink hue – 2 to 3 mins.
Remove the chicken and set it aside.

Heat the remaining tablespoon of safflower oil
over high heat. Add the ginger, garlic, spring onions,
water chestnuts and bamboo shoots; stir-fry for
2 mins. Then add the ham, mushrooms and
peppercorns, and stir-fry for another min. Toss in the
chicken and stir-fry until it is heated through.
Remove pan from heat and stir in soy sauce and
sesame oil. Arrange the lettuce leaves on a platter,
spoon the mixture onto them and serve.

Sautéed Chicken Breasts with Liver and Grapes

Serves 4

Working (and total) time: about 40 minutes

Calories 295

Protein 32g

Cholesterol 210mg

Total fat 11g

Saturated fat 3g

Sodium 215mg

4	chicken breasts, skinned and boned (about 500 g/1 lb)	4
5 g	unsalted butter	$\frac{1}{6}$ oz
1 tbsp	safflower oil	1 tbsp
$\frac{1}{4}$ tsp	salt	$\frac{1}{4}$ tsp
	freshly ground black pepper	
12.5 cl	Madeira	4 fl oz
45 g	shallots, finely chopped	$1\frac{1}{2}$ oz
$\frac{1}{2}$ tsp	crushed mustard seeds	$\frac{1}{2}$ tsp

1 tsp	fresh thyme, or $\frac{1}{4}$ tsp dried thyme	1 tsp
125 g	chicken livers	4 oz
125 g	seedless grapes, cut in half	4 oz
2 tbsp	soured cream	2 tbsp
2 tsp	plain low-fat yogurt	2 tsp
1 tsp	cornflour, mixed with 1 tbsp fresh lime juice	1 tsp
1 tbsp	chopped parsley	1 tbsp

Heat the butter and 1 teaspoon of the oil in a heavy frying pan over medium-high heat. Cook the chicken on one side until lightly browned – about 4 minutes. Turn the pieces over and sprinkle them with the salt and pepper. Cook for 3 minutes on the second side, then remove the breasts, place on a heated platter, and set aside.

Pour the madeira into the pan and simmer to reduce it by half – about 3 minutes. Add the shallots, mustard seeds and thyme, and simmer for 2 or 3 minutes more. Pour the sauce over the chicken, scraping out the pan deposits with it.

Wipe the pan with a paper towel. Heat the remaining 2 teaspoons of the oil in the pan over medium-high heat, and sauté the chicken livers, turning occasionally, until they brown – about 6 minutes. Reduce the heat to low, return the chicken breasts and their sauce to the pan, and add the grapes. Stir the soured cream and yogurt into the cornflour-lime juice mixture, then pour it into the pan. Simmer until the chicken is cooked through – about 5 minutes. Garnish the chicken with the chopped parsley and serve immediately.

Sugested accompaniments: rice pilaff; green beans.

Chicken Cutlets with Herbs and Tomato Sauce

Serves 4

Working time: about 30 minutes

Total time: about 30 minutes

Calories 280

Protein 30g

Cholesterol 70mg

Total fat 10g

Saturated fat 2g

Sodium 325mg

	chicken breasts, skinned and boned (about 500 g/1 lb), pounded to about 1 cm ($\frac{1}{2}$ inch) thickness	4	**1 tbsp each**	finely chopped fresh tarragon, basil and parsley, mixed, plus a few sprigs for garnish	**1 tbsp each**
	garlic clove, finely chopped	1	**$\frac{1}{4}$ tsp**	salt	**$\frac{1}{4}$ tsp**
	large tomatoes, skinned, seeded and coarsely chopped	2	**$\frac{1}{4}$ tsp**	freshly ground white pepper	**$\frac{1}{4}$ tsp**
tbsp	virgin olive oil	1 tbsp	**45 g**	dry breadcrumbs	**1$\frac{1}{2}$ oz**
2.5 cl	unsalted chicken stock	4 fl oz	**2**	egg whites	**2**
tsp	tarragon vinegar	$\frac{3}{4}$ tsp	**1 tbsp**	safflower oil	**1 tbsp**

To prepare the sauce, cook the garlic and tomatoes in the olive oil over medium-high heat in a small saucepan, stirring occasionally, until soft – about 5 minutes. Add the stock, the vinegar and 2 tablespoons of the herb mixture, and bring to the boil. Reduce the heat, cover and simmer for 5 minutes. Purée the sauce in a food processor or blender and return to the pan to keep warm.

Meanwhile, sprinkle the salt and pepper over the breasts. Mix the remaining tablespoon of herbs with the breadcrumbs on a large plate. In a small bowl, whisk the egg whites vigorously

and dip the breasts in the whites, then in the breadcrumb mixture.

Heat the safflower oil in a large, heavy frying pan over medium-high heat and sauté the chicken on one side until lightly brown – about 3 minutes. Turn the breasts, cover the pan loosely, and sauté until they feel firm but springy to the touch – about 4 minutes more. Transfer the breasts to a heated platter and spoon the sauce over them. Garnish with sprigs of herbs.

Suggested accompaniment: corn on the cob.

Chicken Breasts Sautéed with Coriander

Serves 4

Working time: about 30 minutes

Total time: about 30 minutes

Calories
205

Protein
29g

Cholesterol
75mg

Total fat
7g

Saturated fat
2g

Sodium
235mg

4	chicken breasts, skinned and boned (about 500 g/1 lb)	4
1 tbsp	safflower oil	**1 tbsp**
	freshly ground black pepper	
¼ tsp	salt	**¼ tsp**
8 cl	plain low-fat yogurt	**3 fl oz**
2 tbsp	single cream	**2 tbsp**
1 tsp	cornflour, mixed with 1 tbsp water	**1 tsp**
17.5 cl	unsalted chicken stock	**6 fl oz**
2 tbsp	fresh lemon juice	**2 tbsp**
2	garlic cloves, finely chopped	**2**
2 tbsp	finely chopped shallot	**2 tbsp**
1	small tomato, skinned, seeded and chopped	**1**
20 g	fresh coriander leaves, coarsely chopped, 4 leaves reserved for garnish	**¾ oz**

In a heavy frying pan, heat the oil over medium-high heat. Sauté the chicken breasts on one side for 5 minutes, then turn them and sprinkle them with the pepper and half of the salt. Sauté on the second side until they are firm but springy to the touch – about 4 minutes. Transfer the chicken to a heated platter and keep it warm.

In a small bowl, stir the yogurt and cream into the cornflour mixture. Put the stock and lemon juice in the pan; add the garlic and shallot, reduce the heat to low, and simmer for 30 seconds. Stir in the tomato, the yogurt mixture and the remaining salt. Cook over low heat for 1 minute, then add the chopped coriander. Pour the sauce over the chicken and garnish each breast with a fresh coriander leaf, if desired.

Suggested accompaniment: sautéed courgettes.

Sautéed Chicken Breasts with Raspberry Sauce

Serves 4

Working time: about 30 minutes

Total time: about 40 minutes

Calories 225

Protein 27g

Cholesterol 80mg

Total fat 7g

Saturated fat 3g

Sodium 155mg

4	chicken breasts, skinned and boned (about 500 g/1 lb)	**4**	**12.5 cl**	dry white wine	**4 fl oz**
⅛ tsp.	salt	**⅛ tsp**	**1**	shallot, finely chopped	**1**
	freshly ground black pepper		**125 g**	fresh raspberries	**4 oz**
1 tsp	honey	**1 tsp**	**¼ litre**	unsalted chicken stock	**8 fl oz**
1 tbsp	raspberry vinegar	**1 tbsp**		mint sprigs, for garnish	
15 g	unsalted butter	**½ oz**		(optional)	

Sprinkle the chicken breasts with the salt and pepper and put them on a plate. Stir the honey into the raspberry vinegar and mix well. Dribble this mixture over the breasts and allow them to marinate for 15 minutes.

Preheat the oven to 100°C (200°F or Mark ¼). In a heavy frying pan, melt the butter over medium-high heat, and sauté the breasts until golden – about 4 minutes on each side. Transfer the chicken to a serving platter in the oven to keep warm. Add the wine and shallot to the pan. Reduce the liquid until it barely coats the pan –

there should be about 2 tablespoons. Reserve 12 of the raspberries for a garnish. Add the stock and the remaining raspberries and reduce by half. Purée the mixture in a food processor or blender, then strain it through a fine sieve.

Return the sauce to the pan and bring it to the boil. Spoon it over the chicken and garnish with the reserved raspberries and the mint sprigs, if desired.

Suggested accompaniments: peas; steamed rice.

Chicken with Mustard, Caraway Seeds and Chervil

Serves 4

Working time: about 1 hour

Total time: about 1 hour

Calories 440

Protein 30g

Cholesterol 105mg

Total fat 18g

Saturated fat 8g

Sodium 375mg

4	chicken breasts, skinned and boned (about 500 g/1 lb), pounded to 1 cm (½ inch) thickness	4
⅛ tsp	salt	⅛ tsp
	freshly ground black pepper	
3 tbsp	Dijon mustard	3 tbsp
8 cl	plain low-fat yogurt	3 fl oz
2 tsp	caraway seeds	2 tsp
5 tbsp	chopped fresh chervil or parsley	5 tbsp
90 g	dry breadcrumbs	3 oz
30 g	unsalted butter	1 oz
1 tbsp	safflower oil	1 tbsp
3	tart green apples, cored and cut into 5 mm (¼ inch) slices	3
2 tbsp	aquavit or kümmel (optional)	2 tbsp
12.5 cl	unsweetened apple juice	4 fl oz
1 tbsp	fresh lemon juice	1 tbsp
4 tbsp	double cream	4 tbsp

Sprinkle the chicken with the salt and pepper.

In a small bowl, whisk together the mustard, yogurt, caraway seeds and 4 tablespoons of the chervil or parsley. Generously coat the breasts with the mixture, then coat them with the breadcrumbs. Chill for 30 minutes.

Once the breasts have been chilled, heat 15 g (½ oz) of the butter and the oil in a heavy frying pan over medium heat. Place the breasts in the pan and sauté, turning once, until the crumbs are golden – 6 to 8 minutes.

Heat the remaining butter in a frying pan over medium heat. Toss in the apple slices and cook them for 4 to 5 minutes, turning the slices occasionally. Add the aquavit or kümmel, if using, and simmer to evaporate – 1 to 2 minutes. Add the apple juice, the lemon juice and more pepper, and simmer for 3 to 4 minutes. Push the apples to one side of the pan and whisk in the cream. Cook for 2 minutes more.

To serve, place the chicken on a heated platter, and arrange the apple slices around the breasts. Continue simmering the sauce until it thickens slightly – 2 to 3 minutes. Pour over the chicken and apples, and garnish with the remaining tablespoon of chervil or parsley. Serve immediately.

Chicken Riesling

Serves 4

Working
ime: about
0 minutes

Total time:
about
1 hour

Calories
310

Protein
27g

Cholesterol
80mg

Total fat
11g

Saturated fat
3g

Sodium
365mg

	chicken breasts, skinned and boned	4	90 g	mushrooms, thinly sliced	3 oz
	(about 500 g/1 lb)		35 cl	Riesling wine	12 fl oz
	freshly ground black pepper		1 tbsp	chopped fresh tarragon or	1 tbsp
sp	salt	½ tsp		1 tsp dried tarragon	
bsp	safflower oil	1 tbsp	30 cl	unsalted chicken stock	½ pint
g	unsalted butter	½ oz	2 tsp	cornflour	2 tsp
bsp	finely chopped shallots	2 tbsp	125 g	red grapes, halved and seeded	4 oz

eheat the oven to 100°C (200°F or Mark ¼).
Sprinkle the chicken with the pepper and
teaspoon of the salt. Heat the oil over medium-
gh heat in a large, heavy frying pan. Sauté the
eces in the oil until brown – about 5 minutes
each side. Transfer the chicken to a platter
d cover it with foil.

Add the butter, shallots and mushrooms to the
n, sprinkle with half of the remaining salt, and
uté until the shallots soften – 2 to 3 minutes.
ith a slotted spoon, transfer the mushrooms to
e platter with the chicken, and keep it warm
the oven. Add all but 4 tablespoons of the

Riesling to the pan along with the tarragon, and
reduce the liquid to about 4 tablespoons. Pour
in the stock and reduce by half. Mix the cornflour
with the remaining wine. Reduce the heat so
that the sauce simmers, and stir in the cornflour
mixture and the remaining salt. Add the halved
grapes and cook for 2 minutes. Arrange some of
the mushroom mixture on each breast, and pour
the sauce over all.

Suggested accompaniments: garlic bread; oak
leaf lettuce salad.

Chicken, Aubergine and Tomato Sauté

Serves 4

Working time: about 45 minutes

Total time: about 1 hour

Calories
370
Protein
30g
Cholesterol
75mg
Total fat
19g
Saturated fat
4g
Sodium
205mg

4	chicken breasts, skinned and boned (about 500 g/1 lb)	**4**
2	small aubergines, sliced in 5 mm (¼ inch) thick rounds	**2**
5 g	unsalted butter	**⅙ oz**
4 tbsp	virgin olive oil	**4 tbsp**
	freshly ground black pepper	
¼ tsp	salt	**¼ tsp**
4 tbsp	dry sherry	**4 tbsp**
2 tbsp	fresh lemon juice	**2 tbsp**
1 tsp	fresh thyme, or ¼ tsp dried thyme	**1 t**
30 g	dried mushrooms, rinsed and soaked for 1 hour in ¼ litre (8 fl oz) warm water, the water strained through muslin and reserved	**1**
3	large ripe tomatoes, skinned, thickly sliced in rounds	
1 tbsp	red wine vinegar	**1 tb**
2	garlic cloves, finely chopped	
2	spring onions, finely chopped	

Boil 2 litres (3½ pints) of water; blanch the aubergine in batches for 30 seconds. Remove and drain.

Heat the butter and 1 tbsp of oil in a frying pan over medium-high heat. Sauté chicken on one side until brown. Turn and sprinkle with the pepper and half the salt. Reduce the heat to low and cook for 2 mins. Add the sherry, lemon juice, thyme and 4 tbsps mushroom-soaking water. Simmer, covered, until the pieces feel firm but springy – about 5 mins. Set aside.

Preheat the oven to 100°C (200°F or Mark ¼). Heat 1 tbsp of the remaining oil in a frying pan over medium-high. Sauté the aubergine, ⅓ at a time, in a

single layer until golden-brown, turning once. A ½ tbsp oil before each batch. Cover the bottom of ovenproof serving dish with the slices.

Heat remaining oil over medium-high. Sprinkl the tomato with remaining salt and sauté un softened. Arrange tomatoes on top of aubergin Remove chicken from liquid and place on top; ke dish warm in oven.

Simmer the cooking liquid, with the remaini mushroom liquid, mushrooms, vinegar, garlic and the spring onions, until reduced by half.

Spoon over chicken and garnish with remaini spring onions.

Chicken Paprika with Yogurt

Serves 4

Working time: about 45 minutes

Total time: about 1 hour

Calories 475

Protein 46g

Cholesterol 145mg

Total fat 26g

Saturated fat 9g

Sodium 330mg

1.5 kg	chicken, cut into serving pieces, the legs and breasts skinned	**3 lb**	**1**	garlic clove, finely chopped	**1**
2 tbsp	safflower oil	**2 tbsp**	**¼ litre**	unsalted chicken stock	**8 fl oz**
¼ tsp	salt	**¼ tsp**	**2 tbsp**	paprika	**2 tbsp**
275 g	onions, finely chopped	**9 oz**	**17.5 cl**	plain low-fat yogurt	**6 fl oz**
			17.5 cl	soured cream	**6 fl oz**

In a large, heavy frying pan, heat the oil over medium-high heat. Add as many chicken pieces as will fit without crowding, and sauté them on one side until brown – about 4 minutes. Turn the pieces, sprinkle them with the salt, and sauté until the second sides brown – 3 to 4 minutes more. Transfer the chicken to a plate. Repeat with the remaining pieces.

Reduce the heat to medium low and add the onions and garlic to the oil remaining in the pan. Cook, stirring occasionally, until the onions turn translucent – about 10 minutes. Stir in the chicken stock and the paprika, and bring the liquid to a simmer.

Return all of the chicken pieces to the pan, reduce the heat to low, and cover. Simmer until the juices run clear when a thigh is pierced with the tip of a sharp knife – about 25 minutes. Transfer the chicken to a heated platter and cover with foil to keep warm.

Skim any fat from the liquid in the pan. Bring the liquid to the boil over medium-high heat and reduce the stock to about half – 3 to 4 minutes. In a small bowl, whisk together the yogurt and soured cream. Stir in a little of the cooking liquid, then reduce the heat to low and whisk the yogurt mixture into the pan. Cook for 1 minute, then pour the sauce over the chicken and serve immediately.

Suggested accompaniments: egg noodles; peas.

Chicken Breasts with Tarragon and Tomato

Serves 4

Working time: about 30 minutes

Total time: about 2 hours and 30 minutes

Calories 225

Protein 27g

Cholesterol 90mg

Total fat 10g

Saturated fat 5g

Sodium 215mg

4	chicken breasts, skinned and boned (about 500 g/1 lb)	**4**
12.5 cl	buttermilk	**4 fl oz**
1 tbsp	fresh lime or lemon juice	**1 tbsp**
1 tbsp	fresh tarragon leaves, or 1 tsp dried tarragon	**1 tbsp**
15 g	unsalted butter	**½ oz**

¼ tsp	salt	**¼ tsp**
2	tomatoes, skinned, seeded, finely chopped	**2**
1	shallot, finely chopped	
	finely ground black pepper	
12.5 cl	single cream	**4 fl oz**

In a wide, shallow bowl, combine the buttermilk, lime or lemon juice, and half of the tarragon. Marinate the chicken in this mixture for 2 hours or overnight. Remove the chicken from the marinade, gently wiping off as much liquid as possible with your fingers.

In a heavy frying pan, heat the butter over medium heat. Cook the chicken breasts on one side for 5 minutes. Turn the pieces over, sprinkle them with the salt, and cook for 5 minutes more. Remove them from the pan and keep them warm.

In the same pan, cook the tomatoes, shallot, pepper and the remaining tarragon over medium heat until the tomato liquid evaporates – about 3 minutes. Stir in the cream, reduce the heat to low, and simmer for 1 minute, stirring. Cut the breasts into slices and arrange them on a serving platter. Pour the sauce over just before serving.

Suggested accompaniments: julienned carrots, steamed courgettes.

Chicken with Broccoli, Red Onions and Cashew Nuts

Serves 4

Working time: about 25 minutes

Total time: about 35 minutes

Calories 350

Protein 27g

Cholesterol 55mg

Total fat 20g

Saturated fat 3g

Sodium 520mg

3	chicken breasts, (about 350 g/12 oz), skinned, boned and sliced into 7.5 cm (3 inch) strips about 1 cm (⅓ inch) wide	**3**
¼ tsp	salt	**¼ tsp**
¾ tsp	freshly ground white pepper	**¾ tsp**
1¼ tbsp	peanut oil	**1¼ tbsp**
3 tbsp	safflower oil	**3 tbsp**
5	slices fresh ginger root, crushed	**5**
5	large garlic cloves, peeled and crushed lightly so remain whole	**5**
2	carrots, thinly sliced diagonally	**2**

250 g	broccoli, florets separated, stems trimmed and thinly sliced diagonally	**8 oz**
4–6	water chestnuts, sliced (optional)	**4–6**
1	red onion, chopped into squares	**1**
2 tbsp	unsalted cashew nuts	**2 tbsp**
3	spring onions, sliced diagonally	**3**
12.5 cl	unsalted chicken stock	**4 fl oz**
2 tbsp	cornflour, mixed with 1 tbsp low-sodium soy sauce, or shoyu, and 1 tbsp dry sherry	**2 tbsp**
¼ tsp	dark sesame oil	**¼ tsp**

Combine chicken breasts, with ¼ tsp salt and ½ tsp pepper.

Heat a wok over medium-high heat. Mix peanut and safflower oils together. When the wok is hot, slowly pour in 2 tbsp of the blended oil to coat the surface.

Stir-fry the ginger and garlic for about 30 secs. Add the chicken and stir-fry, until the meat turns white.

Discard the ginger and garlic. Transfer chicken to a plate, set it aside; do not discard the oil.

Pour 1 more tbsp of the blended oil into the wok. Add broccoli and carrot, sprinkle with remaining salt and pepper, stir-fry until the oil has coated all. Pour in the remaining oil, then add water chestnuts, onion, cashews and ⅔ of the spring onions. Stir-fry for 1 to 2 mins.

Return the chicken to the wok and stir-fry the chicken and vegetables together. Push the contents to the sides and pour the stock into the centre. Stir the cornflour mixture into the stock and cook until thickened. Coat the chicken and vegetables evenly with the sauce. Add sesame oil and stir well. Serve with spring onion garnish.

Chicken Breasts with Apricots, Bourbon and Pecans

Serves 4

Working time: about 30 minutes

Total time: about 8 hours

Calories 405

Protein 29g

Cholesterol 75mg

Total fat 11g

Saturated fat 2g

Sodium 250mg

4	chicken breasts, skinned and boned (about 500 g/1 lb)	4
250 g	dried apricots	8 oz
8 cl	bourbon whiskey	3 fl oz
17.5 cl	unsalted chicken stock	6 fl oz
5 g	unsalted butter	⅙ oz
1 tsp	safflower oil	1 tsp
¼ tsp	salt	¼ tsp
	freshly ground black pepper	

1	shallot, finely chopped	1
1 tsp	tomato paste	1 tsp
2 tsp	grainy mustard	2 tsp
30 g	pecans, toasted in a 180°C (350°F or Mark 4) oven, then crushed with a rolling pin	1 oz
1	spring onion, cut into 5 cm (2 inch) long pieces thinly sliced	1

Marinate the apricots in the bourbon and a third of the stock for 8 hours or overnight. Alternatively, bring the bourbon and a third of the stock to the boil, then turn off the heat and steep the apricots in the liquid until they soften – about 10 minutes.

Heat the butter and the oil in a heavy frying pan over medium-high heat. Sauté the chicken breasts on one side until lightly coloured – about 4 minutes. Turn them over and sprinkle with the salt and pepper. Sauté them on the second side for 4 minutes. Drain the bourbon and stock from the apricots, and pour it over the chicken. Add the remaining stock, reduce the heat to low and

cook until the chicken feels firm but springy to the touch – about 5 minutes. Transfer to a plate and cover with aluminium foil to keep it warm.

Add the apricots and shallot to the pan and simmer for 2 minutes. Whisk in the tomato paste and mustard and simmer for 3 minutes, stirring occasionally. Return the breasts to the pan for 1 or 2 minutes to heat through.

Arrange the chicken and the apricots on a warmed platter. Spoon the sauce over chicken and sprinkle with the pecans and spring onion.

Suggested accompaniment: steamed Swiss chard.

Stir-Fried Chicken with Red Cabbage and Chilies

Serves 4

Working
and total)
me: about
5 minutes

Calories
265

Protein
23g

Cholesterol
55mg

Total fat
10g

Saturated fat
1g

Sodium
355mg

	chicken breasts, skinned and boned (about 350 g/12 oz) cut into 1 cm (½ inch) wide strips	**3**	**150 g**	French beans	**5 oz**	
tbsp	finely chopped stoned prunes	**4 tbsp**	**1 tbsp**	low-sodium soy sauce, or naturally fermented shoyu	**1 tbsp**	
	garlic cloves, finely chopped	**2**	**1**	small red cabbage, cored and cut into 5 cm (2 inch) strips	**1**	
2	large dried red chili peppers, seeded, cut into very thin strips, or ½ tsp crushed red pepper flakes	**1–2**	**¼ tsp**	salt	**¼ tsp**	
tbsp	safflower oil	**2 tbsp**	**7**	spring onions, trimmed, halved lengthwise and cut into 5 cm (2 inch) strips	**7**	

ombine the prunes, garlic, chilies or crushed
d pepper flakes, and ½ teaspoon of the oil in
large, shallow dish. Add the chicken and
arinate for at least 30 minutes, turning
'casionally to coat the meat. Blanch the beans
r 1 minute in ½ litre (16 fl oz) of boiling water.
fresh the beans under cold water, place them
a bowl, and add the soy sauce. Set aside to
arinate, turning occasionally to coat the beans.
Heat a wok or large, heavy frying pan over
gh heat. Pour in an additional tablespoon of
l and stir-fry the cabbage with the salt until the
bbage wilts – about 3 minutes. Add the beans

with the soy sauce and half the spring onions.
Continue stir-frying for 3 minutes, stirring and
tossing. Empty the wok or pan into a large bowl.

Return the pan to the heat. Pour in the
remaining oil and immediately add the chicken
and its marinade along with the rest of the spring
onions. Reduce the heat to medium high and stir
and toss until the chicken is cooked – about
4 minutes. Add the cabbage mixture, mix well,
and serve immediately.

Suggested accompaniments: saffron rice; firm
tofu sautéed with soy sauce.

Poached Chicken with Fennel

Serves 6

Working time: about 30 minutes

Total time: about 1 hour

Calories **340**

Protein **29g**

Cholesterol **95mg**

Total fat **11g**

Saturated fat **4g**

Sodium **515mg**

6	chicken legs, skinned	6
1 tbsp	black peppercorns	1 tbsp
2	garlic cloves, peeled	2
¼ litre	anise-flavoured liquer	8 fl oz
¾ litre	unsalted chicken stock	1¼ pints
1	onion, thinly sliced	1
½ tsp	fennel seeds	½ tsp
1 tsp	salt	1 tsp
1	stick celery, cut into 7.5 cm (3 inch) strips about (¼ inch) 5 mm wide	1

2	large fennel bulbs, the tough outer layer and feathery green tops trimmed and reserved, the bulbs cut lengthwise into 6 pieces	
1	bay leaf	
2	large lettuce leaves, preferably cos	
250 g	baby carrots, tops removed, peeled	8
15 g	unsalted butter	½
	freshly ground black pepper	

Crush the peppercorns and the garlic and mash them into a paste. Spread over each chicken leg.

Bring the liqueur to the boil in a fireproof casserole. Add the chicken and coat with the liqueur. Add the stock, onion, fennel seeds and salt; if necessary, add water or stock to just cover the chicken. Return to the boil. Reduce the heat and simmer for 15 minutes.

Make a bouquet garni: wrap the tough outer layer and trimmings from the fennel, the celery strips and bay leaf in the lettuce, and tie the bundle with string. Place this in the casserole.

At the end of the 15 minutes, add the fennel pieces, pressing them into the liquid. Cover and simmer for 5 minutes more. Add the carrots cooking, uncovered, until juices run clear when a chicken thigh is pierced with the tip of a sharp knife – 7 to 10 minutes. Transfer the chicken legs and the vegetables to a warmed serving platter.

Reduce the poaching liquid over high heat to about 30 cl (½ pint). Remove the bouquet garni. Whisk the butter and some pepper into the sauce and pour it over the chicken and vegetables garnish with the feathery fennel tops.

Poached Chicken Strips in Gingered Orange Sauce

Serves 6

Working
time: about
45 minutes

Total time:
about
1 hour and
30 minutes

Calories
180

Protein
20g

Cholesterol
55mg

Total fat
5g

Saturated fat
2g

Sodium
185mg

	chicken breasts, skinned and boned (about 500 g/1 lb), cut into 1 cm (½ inch) strips	**4**		30 g/¾ to 1 oz), peeled and cut into chunks	
¼ tsp	salt	**¼ tsp**	**2**	navel oranges, the rind julienned and the flesh segmented	**2**
	freshly ground black pepper		**¼ tsp**	aromatic bitters	**¼ tsp**
¼ litre	fresh orange juice	**8 fl oz**	**1 tsp**	whisky	**1 tsp**
¾ litre	unsalted chicken stock	**1¼ pints**	**30 g**	cream cheese	**1 oz**
4–5 cm	fresh ginger root (25 to	**1½–2 inches**	**1 tbsp**	cornflour	**1 tbsp**

Marinate the chicken in the refrigerator for 1 hour in the orange juice, with ½ of the salt and some pepper.

Lift the chicken out of the marinade. Pour the marinade into a pan. Add ½ litre (16 fl oz) of the stock, remaining salt and some pepper. Squeeze the ginger through a garlic press into the pan. Bring to boil, reduce heat, cover, simmer for 4 mins. Remove from heat and let the ginger steep for 15 mins.

Meanwhile, put the orange rind in a pan. Cover with 12.5 cl (4 fl oz) of the stock, the bitters and the whisky. Cook briskly until almost all the liquid has evaporated; set aside. In another pan, pour the remaining stock over the orange

segments; cover and set aside.

Return the gingery liquid to the boil. Add the chicken, reduce the heat. Simmer until the chicken feels firm but springy to touch – about 1 minute. Remove the chicken to a warmed platter.

In a bowl, soften the cheese with the back of a spoon. Stir in the cornflour. Pour about 12.5 cl (4 fl oz) of the hot liquid into the bowl and whisk. Add same again of liquid, then pour mixture back into the pan and cook, whisking, until the sauce thickens – 2 or 3 mins. Spoon sauce over chicken. Heat orange segments in stock and arrange round the chicken. Garnish with orange rind.

Red Pepper and Chicken Spirals

Serves 4

Working time: about 30 minutes

Total time: about 45 minutes

Calories 250

Protein 28g

Cholesterol 70mg

Total fat 11g

Saturated fat 2g

Sodium 535mg

4	chicken breasts, skinned, boned, the long triangular fillets removed and reserved for another use, lightly pounded to 5 mm ($\frac{1}{4}$ inch) thickness	**4**
$\frac{1}{4}$ tsp	salt	**$\frac{1}{4}$ tsp**
$\frac{1}{2}$ tsp	crushed Sichuan peppercorns, or $\frac{1}{4}$ tsp crushed black peppercorns	**$\frac{1}{2}$ tsp**
3	spring onions, blanched for 30 secs, drained, cooled, patted dry, and halved lengthwise	**3**
1	cucumber, peeled, halved lengthwise, seeded, cut into 5 mm ($\frac{1}{4}$ inch) wide strips, blanched for 30 seconds, drained, cooled and patted dry	**1**
1	sweet red pepper, seeded, deribbed, cut into 1 cm ($\frac{1}{2}$ inch) strips, blanched for 2 minutes, drained, and patted dry	
2 tbsp	safflower oil	**2 tbsp**

Mirin Sauce

3 tbsp	low-sodium soy sauce, or naturally fermented shoyu	**3 tbsp**
1 tbsp	sugar	**1 tbsp**
2 tbsp	mirin, or dry sherry	**2 tbsp**
2 tsp	rice vinegar	**2 tsp**
$\frac{1}{2}$ tsp	crushed Sichuan peppercorns, or $\frac{1}{4}$ tsp crushed black peppercorns	**$\frac{1}{2}$ tsp**

Combine the sauce ingredients with 3 tbsp water. Set aside.

Sprinkle the chicken with the salt and crushed peppercorns. Cut the spring onions, cucumber strips and pepper strips to fit inside the breasts. Arrange some spring onions, cucumber and pepper strips across the grain of the meat at the wide edge of each breast. Roll up the chicken and fasten with a small skewer.

Heat the oil in a frying pan over medium heat and sauté the rolls, turning, until golden – about 4 minutes. Remove the chicken and pour in the sauce, stirring, being sure to scrape up any brown bits from the bottom. Return the chicken cover, and simmer for 8 minutes, turning once.

Transfer the chicken to a heated platter, remove the skewers, and cut into slices. Pour the sauce over the slices and serve immediately.

Poached Chicken with Black Bean Onion Sauce

Serves 4

Working time: about 30 minutes

Total time: about 1 hour and 30 minutes

Calories 485

Protein 45g

Cholesterol 125mg

Total fat 18g

Saturated fat 4g

Sodium 235mg

1.5 kg	chicken, trussed	**3 lb**
2 tbsp	safflower oil	**2 tbsp**
3	onions, sliced	**3**
1 tbsp	flour	**1 tbsp**
2 tsp	fermented black beans, rinsed well	**2 tsp**
2	garlic cloves, finely chopped	**2**
¼ litre	dry white wine	**8 fl oz**
¾ litre	unsalted beef stock	**1¼ pints**
2 tbsp	brandy	**2 tbsp**
1	small potato, peeled and cut into chunks	**1**
	freshly ground black pepper	
15 g	unsalted butter, cut into pieces	**½ oz**

Pour the oil into a casserole set over medium-low heat, and stir in the onions. Cover, cook, stirring occasionally, until the onions are greatly reduced and quite limp – about 30 minutes.

Uncover the casserole and stir in the flour, beans and garlic. Cook, stirring, for 1 minute. Add the wine, the stock, the brandy, potato and some pepper. Lower the chicken into the casserole. If necessary, pour in additional water to cover.

Place a sheet of foil over the chicken and cover the casserole. Poach over medium-low heat, turning several times, until juices run clear when a thigh is pierced with the tip of a knife – about 45 minutes. Transfer chicken to a carving board and cover with foil to keep warm.

To prepare the sauce, first skim the fat off the cooking liquid. Set a strainer or colander over a bowl and pour the liquid through it. Reserve 4 tablespoons of the onions. Transfer the drained potato pieces and the remaining onions to a food processor or blender, add 12.5 cl (4 fl oz) of the strained cooking liquid, and purée the mixture until smooth. Pour in an additional ¼ litre (8 fl oz) of the cooking liquid and purée again until smooth.

Pour the sauce into a small pan and warm it gently. Remove from the heat; swirl in the butter.

Carve the chicken into serving pieces. Spoon sauce over pieces and scatter reserved onions over them. Pass remaining sauce separately.

Cranberried Chicken

Serves 4

Working time: about 20 minutes

Total time: about 3 hours

Calories
610

Protein
42g

Cholesterol
133mg

Total fat
13g

Saturated fat
5g

Sodium
133mg

1.5 kg	chicken cut into serving pieces, skinned	**3 lb**
1.75 litres	cranberry or apple juice	**3 pints**
30 g	basil, lightly crushed to bruise the leaves, or 1½ tbsp dried basil	**1 oz**
1	onion, sliced	**1**

250 g	cranberries	**8 oz**
125 g	sugar	**4 oz**
2 tbsp	raspberry vinegar	**2 tbsp**
1 tsp	cornflour, mixed with 2 tbsp water	**1 tsp**
15 g	unsalted butter, cut into pieces	**½ oz**

In a large, non-reactive saucepan, simmer 1.25 litres (2 pints) of the cranberry juice with the basil and onion for 10 minutes. Let the liquid cool, then add the chicken pieces. Marinate for 2 hours at room temperature or overnight in the refrigerator, turning the pieces occasionally.

If needed, pour in enough water to cover the chicken pieces. Bring the liquid to a simmer and reduce the heat. Partially cover the pan. Poach the chicken gently, skimming the foam from the surface, until the juices run clear when a thigh is pierced with the tip of a sharp knife – 15 to 20 minutes.

Simmer the cranberries in the rest of the juice with the sugar until they almost burst – about 7 minutes. Drain and discard the liquid.

Transfer the chicken to a heated serving platter and cover it to keep it warm. Strain the poaching liquid and return it to the pot. Add the vinegar and bring the liquid to the boil. Cook over medium-high heat until the liquid is reduced to about 35 cl (12 fl oz) – 15 to 25 minutes. Stir in the cornflower mixture and the cooked cranberries, and simmer until the sauce has thickened slightly – 2 or 3 minutes. Remove the pot from the heat and swirl in the butter. Spoon some of the sauce over the chicken and pass the rest separately.

Suggested accompaniments: wild rice; braised fennel.

Chicken Poached in Milk and Curry

Serves 4

Working time: about 15 minutes

Total time: about 1 hour and 15 minutes

Calories **450**

Protein **52g**

Cholesterol **160mg**

Total fat **20g**

Saturated fat **10g**

Sodium **490mg**

5 kg	chicken, wings reserved for another use, the rest skinned and cut into serving pieces	**3 lb**	**3**	garlic cloves, crushed	**3**
			1 tsp	curry powder	**1 tsp**
			½ tsp	salt	**½ tsp**
litre	milk	**1¼ pints**		freshly ground black pepper	
	large sweet onions, thinly sliced	**2**	**150 g**	shelled peas	**5 oz**
-5	bay leaves	**4–5**	**15 g**	unsalted butter	**½ oz**
tsp	fresh thyme, or ½ tsp dried thyme	**2 tsp**			

a saucepan over medium heat, mix the milk, nions, bay leaves, thyme, garlic, curry powder, lt and a little pepper. Bring just to a simmer, en immediately remove from the heat. Allow stand for 30 minutes; after 15 minutes, preheat e oven to 175°C (325°F or Mark 3).

Arrange the chicken in a baking dish large nough to hold them snugly. Bring the milk-nd-onion mixture to a simmer again and pour over the chicken. Set the saucepan aside; do ot wash it. Drape the onion slices over any hicken pieces that protrude from the liquid so at the chicken will not dry out during cooking. ut the dish in the oven and poach the chicken ntil the juices run clear when a thigh is pierced

with the tip of a sharp knife – 35 to 40 minutes.

Take the dish from the oven and turn the oven off. Remove the chicken pieces from the liquid and distribute them among four shallow serving bowls. Strain the poaching liquid into the saucepan, and use some onion slices to garnish each piece of chicken. Discard the remaining onions. Keep the bowls warm in the oven.

Cook the liquid in the pan over medium heat until it is reduced by about one quarter. Add the peas and cook them until tender – about 5 minutes. Remove the pan from the heat and whisk in the butter. Pour some of the sauce and peas over the chicken in each bowl and serve immediately.

Chicken Fan with Basil-Tomato Sauce

Serves 4

Working time: about 30 minutes

Total time: about 30 minutes

Calories 210

Protein 29g

Cholesterol 75mg

Total fat 6g

Saturated fat 1g

Sodium 90mg

4	chicken breasts, skinned and boned (about 500 g/1 lb)	4
½ litre	unsalted chicken stock	16 fl oz
125 g	fresh basil leaves	4 oz
1	garlic clove	1
2 tsp	mayonnaise	2 tsp
1	tomato, skinned, seeded and chopped	1

In a pot large enough to hold the chicken breasts snugly, simmer the stock with 30 g (1 oz) of the basil leaves over medium-low heat for 5 minutes. Add the breasts to the stock, cover, and poach gently for 8 minutes.

Turn the breasts over and poach until they feel firm but springy to the touch – about 4 minutes more.

Meanwhile, chop the garlic in a food processor or blender. Add the remaining basil along with 12.5 cl (4 fl oz) of water, and purée the mixture. Pour the purée into a sieve and lightly press it with a spoon to remove excess water. To prepare

the sauce, scrape the purée into a small bowl and stir in the mayonnaise and half of the chopped tomato.

Lift the chicken breasts from their liquid and pat dry. Cut each piece diagonally into slices and spread them in a fan pattern on individual serving plates. Spoon about 1½ tablespoons of the sauce at the base of each fan. Scatter the remaining chopped tomato over the sauce.

Suggested accompaniment: spaghetti squash or vegetable marrow with Parmesan cheese.

Chicken Legs with Celery, Shallots and Red Onion

Serves 4

Working time: about 20 minutes

Total time: about 50 minutes

Calories 300

Protein 28g

Cholesterol 100mg

Total fat 17g

Saturated fat 5g

Sodium 345mg

	whole chicken legs, skinned	4	**¼ litre**	unsalted chicken stock	**8 fl oz**	
tsp	salt	**¼ tsp**	**½ tsp**	celery seeds	**½ tsp**	
	freshly ground black pepper		**15 g**	unsalted butter	**½ oz**	
tbsp	safflower oil	**2 tbsp**	**½**	large red onion, thinly sliced	**½**	
	celery sticks, sliced diagonally into 5 mm (¼ inch) wide slices	4	**2 tsp**	cornflour, mixed with 1 tbsp water	**2 tsp**	
tbsp	shallots, halved lengthwise, thinly sliced	**2 tbsp**				

Preheat the oven to 180°C (350°F or Mark 4). Sprinkle the chicken with the salt and pepper. Heat 1 tablespoon of the oil in a large, fireproof casserole over medium-high heat. Brown the legs in the oil for about 2 minutes on each side. Transfer the legs to a plate and set them aside.

Add the remaining tablespoon of oil to the casserole and sauté the celery, stirring frequently, for about 1 minute. Add the shallots and sauté them for another minute, taking care not to brown them. Deglaze the casserole with the stock and stir in the celery seeds. Return the legs to the casserole, bring the liquid to a simmer, and cover. Cook the chicken in the oven until the juices run clear when a thigh is pierced with the tip of a sharp knife – about 25 minutes.

Meanwhile, melt the butter in a heavy frying pan over medium-low heat, and sauté the onion until translucent – about 10 minutes. Set aside.

Remove the legs from the casserole, strain the liquid into a saucepan, and reserve the celery. To finish the sauce, bring to a simmer over low heat, stir in the cornflour mixture, and simmer, stirring constantly, until the sauce thickens – about 2 minutes. Spread the celery on a warmed serving platter, pour the sauce over the celery and lay the legs on top. Stew the sautéed onions over the chicken and serve at once.

Spanish-Style Chicken and Saffron Rice

Serves 4

Working time: about 30 minutes

Total time: about 1 hour and 30 minutes

Calories
570

Protein
41g

Cholesterol
105mg

Total fat
20g

Saturated fat
4g

Sodium
410mg

1.25 kg	chicken, skinned, cut into serving pieces	**2½ lb**	
	freshly ground black pepper		
½ tsp	salt	**½ tsp**	
3 tbsp	virgin olive oil	**3 tbsp**	
2	medium onions, thinly sliced	**2**	
175 g	long-grain brown rice	**6 oz**	
12.5 cl	dry white wine	**4 fl oz**	
⅛ tsp	crushed saffron threads	**⅛ tsp**	
35 cl	unsalted chicken stock	**12 fl oz**	

2 tbsp	mildly hot chilies	**2 tbsp**	
⅛ tsp	crushed cumin seeds	**⅛ tsp**	
2	garlic cloves, finely chopped		
2	large ripe tomatoes, skinned, seeded and chopped		
1 each	red and yellow sweet pepper, grilled, skinned, seeded and cut into 2.5 cm (1 inch) strips	**1 each**	
	fresh coriander for garnish (optional)		

Sprinkle the chicken pieces with pepper and ¼ teaspoon of salt. In a lidded fireproof 4 litre (7 pint) casserole, heat 2 tablespoons of the olive oil over medium-high heat. Sauté the chicken until golden-brown – about 4 minutes on each side – and remove to a plate.

Add the remaining tablespoon of olive oil to the casserole and cook the onions over medium heat until translucent – about 10 minutes. Add the brown rice and cook for 2 minutes, stirring constantly to coat the grains thoroughly; pour in

the white wine, bring to the boil, then reduce the heat, cover and simmer until all the liquid has been absorbed – about 8 minutes. Add the saffron to the stock and pour over the rice. Stir in the chilies, cumin seeds, the remaining salt and the garlic. Simmer 15 minutes more and add the tomatoes and chicken, pushing them down into the rice. Cook until the juices run clear when a thigh is pierced with the tip of a sharp knife – about 25 minutes more. Garnish with the pepper strips and coriander.

Orange-Glazed Chicken

Serves 4

Working time: about 20 minutes

Total time: about 1 hour

Calories 455

Protein 40g

Cholesterol 125mg

Total fat 23g

Saturated fat 6g

Sodium 420mg

1.5 kg	chicken, quartered	3 lb	1	navel orange, peeled and segmented, the rind grated	1
½ tsp	salt	½ tsp			
	freshly ground black pepper			**Orange Glaze**	
1 tbsp	safflower oil	1 tbsp	4 tbsp	orange juice	4 tbsp
1	garlic clove, crushed	1	4 tbsp	brown sugar	4 tbsp
¼ litre	unsalted chicken stock	8 fl oz	2 tbsp	cider vinegar	2 tbsp
1 tsp	cornflour, mixed with 1 tbsp water	1 tsp	1 tsp	Dijon mustard	1 tsp

Sprinkle the chicken with the salt and pepper. Heat the oil in a large, heavy frying pan over medium-high heat. Add the chicken pieces and brown them lightly – about 4 minutes on each side. Push the chicken to one side of the pan, add the garlic, and sauté for 15 seconds. Stir in the stock and allow it to come to a simmer. Redistribute the chicken pieces in the pan. Reduce the heat to low and braise until the juices run clear when a thigh is pierced with the tip of a sharp knife – about 25 minutes.

Meanwhile, make the glaze. In a small saucepan over medium-low heat, combine the orange juice, brown sugar, vinegar and mustard.

Bring the mixture to a simmer and cook it for 3 minutes.

When the chicken is cooked, transfer it to a grill pan. Skim off and discard the fat from the braising liquid in the frying pan. Bring the liquid to a simmer, stir in the cornflour mixture and the grated orange rind, and simmer for 5 minutes.

Brush the chicken pieces with the glaze and place them under the grill for a few minutes to brown. Garnish the chicken with the orange segments and pour the sauce over them.

Suggested accompaniment: sugar snap peas.

29

Saffron Chicken Stew

Serves 4

Working time: about 20 minutes

Total time: about 1 hour and 10 minutes

Calories 595

Protein 37g

Cholesterol 90mg

Total fat 17g

Saturated fat 3g

Sodium 685mg

4	chicken legs, skinned, cut into thighs and drumsticks	4
1	garlic clove, halved	1
¼ tsp	freshly ground black pepper	¼ tsp
½ tsp	salt	½ tsp
2 tbsp	safflower oil	2 tbsp
1	aubergine (about 350 g/12 oz), cut into 2.5 cm (1 inch) cubes	1
250 g	yellow squash, cut into 5 cm (2 inch) cubes	8 oz
6	spring onions	6
3	celery sticks, trimmed and cut into 1 cm (½ inch) pieces	3
125 g	baby carrots	4 oz
1	large ripe tomato, skinned, seeded and coarsely chopped	1
½ tsp	fennel seeds	½ tsp
⅛ tsp	saffron threads, crumbled	⅛ tsp
1	bay leaf	1
1 tsp	fresh thyme, or ¼ tsp dried thyme	1 tsp
¼ litre	dry vermouth	8 fl oz
8	red potatoes (about 750 g/1½ lb), with a band peeled from the middle of each	8
4 tbsp	coarsely chopped parsley	4 tbsp
8	slices French bread, toasted	8

Rub the chicken with the garlic and reserve it; sprinkle chicken with the pepper and ¼ tsp salt. Heat 1 tbsp oil in a 6 litre (10 pint) pan over medium heat. Brown the chicken for about 3 mins on each side. Remove and drain on paper towels.

Add the remaining oil to the pan. Add the garlic, aubergine, squash and the remaining salt, and sauté lightly over high heat for about 1 min. Pour in 1.5 litres (2½ pints) of water. Return the chicken to the pan. Add the spring onions, celery, carrots, tomato, fennel seeds, saffron, bay leaf, thyme and vermouth, and bring to the boil. Reduce the heat and simmer gently for about 30 mins, skimming off the fat from time to time. Add the potatoes and simmer for 15 mins. The vegetables should be tender. Remove the bay leaf and garlic. Add the parsley and serve the stew in soup bowls, with the toasted French bread.

Braised Chicken with Plums and Lemons

Serves 4

Working time: about 20 minutes

Total time: about 45 minutes

Calories 260

Protein 28g

Cholesterol 90mg

Total fat 11g

Saturated fat 5g

Sodium 170mg

4	chicken breasts, skinned and boned (about 500 g/1 lb)	4
¼ litre	unsalted chicken stock	16 fl oz
4	red plums, blanched in the stock for 1 minute, peeled (skins reserved), halved and stoned	4
2 tsp	sugar	2 tsp
30 g	unsalted butter	1 oz
⅛ tsp	salt	⅛ tsp
	freshly ground black pepper	
2 tbsp	chopped shallots	2 tbsp
8	paper-thin lemon slices	8

In a saucepan over medium heat, cook the plum skins in the chicken stock until the liquid is reduced to 12.5 cl (4 fl oz). Strain the stock and return it to the pan. Reduce the heat to low, and add the plum halves and sugar. Simmer the mixture for 1 minute, then remove it from the heat and set aside. Preheat the oven to 190°C (375°F or Mark 5).

In a shallow fireproof casserole over medium heat, melt the butter. Lay the breasts in the casserole and sauté them lightly on one side for about 2 minutes. Turn them over, salt and pepper the cooked side, and add the shallots. Place the plum halves cut side down between the breasts. Pour the stock into the casserole and arrange two lemon slices on each breast.

Put the uncovered casserole in the oven. Cook until the chicken feels firm but springy to the touch – about 10 minutes. Remove the casserole from the oven and lift out the plums and breasts with a slotted spoon. Place them on a warmed platter and return the lemon slices to the sauce. Cover the chicken and plums with foil to keep them warm. Simmer the sauce over medium-high heat until it is reduced to about 4 tablespoons – 5 to 7 minutes. Put the lemon slices back on top of the breasts and arrange the plums around them. Pour the sauce over all and serve.

Suggested accompaniment: mashed swedes and potatoes.

Chicken with Orange and Onion

Serves 8

Working
time: about
30 minutes

Total time:
about
1 hour and
15 minutes

Calories
370

Protein
42g

Cholesterol
125mg

Total fat
14g

Saturated fat
3g

Sodium
255mg

Two	chickens, wings removed,	Two
1.5 kg	quartered and skinned	3 lb
2 tbsp	flour	2 tbsp
½ tsp	salt	½ tsp
	freshly ground black pepper	
2 tbsp	safflower oil	2 tbsp
1	orange, rind only, julienned	1

3	onions, thinly sliced	3
2 tsp	fresh thyme, or ½ tsp dried thyme	2 tsp
30 cl	fresh orange juice	½ pint
2 tbsp	fresh lemon juice	2 tbsp
1 tbsp	honey	1 tbsp
17.5 cl	dry white wine	6 fl oz

Dust the chicken pieces with the flour. Sprinkle them with ¼ teaspoon of the salt and some of the pepper.

In a large, heavy frying pan, heat the oil over medium-high heat and sauté the chicken in several batches until golden-brown – about 5 minutes on each side. Transfer the pieces to a 23 by 33 cm (9 by 13 inch) baking dish and scatter the orange rind over them.

Preheat the oven to 180°C (350°F or Mark 4). Over medium-low heat, cook the onions in the oil in the pan, stirring occasionally, until they are translucent – about 10 minutes. Stir in the thyme

and the remaining salt and spread the mixture over the chicken pieces.

Pour the orange and lemon juice, honey and wine into the pan. Bring the liquid to the boil and reduce it to about ¼ litre (8 fl oz). Pour the liquid over the chicken. Cook the pieces uncovered in the oven, basting once with the liquid, until the juices run clear when a thigh is pierced with the tip of a sharp knife – about 35 minutes.

Suggested accompaniments: new potatoes cooked in their jackets; steamed celery.

Braised Chicken with Red and Green Apples

Serves 4

Working time: about 30 minutes

Total time: about 1 hour and 15 minutes

Calories 535

Protein 40g

Cholesterol 135mg

Total fat 27g

Saturated fat 8g

Sodium 560mg

1.5 kg	chicken, cut into serving pieces	**3 lb**
¼ tsp	freshly ground black pepper	**¼ tsp**
¾ tsp	salt	**¾ tsp**
5 g	unsalted butter	**⅙ oz**
1 tbsp	safflower oil	**1 tbsp**
1	small onion, coarsely chopped	**1**
1	celery stick, coarsely chopped	**1**
½	carrot, coarsely chopped	**½**
1	garlic clove, crushed	**1**
1½	cooking apples, peeled, thinly sliced	**1½**
1 tbsp	chopped fresh tarragon	**1 tbsp**

¼ litre	dry vermouth	**8 fl oz**
¼ litre	unsalted chicken stock	**8 fl oz**
2 tsp	plain low-fat yogurt	**2 tsp**
2 tbsp	double cream	**2 tbsp**
	Apple Garnish	
1 tbsp	sugar	**1 tbsp**
1 tsp	tarragon vinegar	**1 tsp**
3 tbsp	unsalted chicken stock	**3 tbsp**
½ each	unpeeled firm red and tart green apple, quartered and cut into 5 mm (¼ inch) slices	**½ each**

Sprinkle the chicken with the pepper and ½ tsp salt. Melt the fats in a large pan over medium-high and sauté pieces on both sides until golden. Drain on paper towels.

Pour off all but 1 tbsp fat. Add the vegetables, garlic, apples and tarragon, and cook until onions are translucent.

Add the vermouth and reduce by ⅔. Return the chicken to the pan, add the stock, and bring to the boil. Reduce the heat, cover and simmer until the juices run clear when a thigh is pierced with a sharp knife – about 20 mins. With a slotted spoon, transfer the contents of the pan to a heated serving platter and keep warm.

Pour 35 cl (12 fl oz) of the liquid into a pan. Skim off the fat, then simmer and reduce by ½. Add the remaining salt, the yogurt and the cream to the sauce. Gently heat the sugar, stirring, until it caramelizes. Carefully add the vinegar and stock, and cook until sugar melts again and liquid becomes syrupy. Toss the apples in the liquid. Serve with the chicken and pass the sauce separately.

Chicken Braised with Haricot Beans and Tomatoes

Serves 6

Working time: about 1 hour

Total time: about 1 day

Calories 505

Protein 42g

Cholesterol 100mg

Total fat 19g

Saturated fat 4g

Sodium 520mg

1.75 kg	skinless chicken pieces	**3½ lb**
500 g	dried haricot beans, soaked overnight in water and drained	**1 lb**
½ tsp	salt	**½ tsp**
	freshly ground black pepper	
1 tbsp	fresh thyme, or ¾ tsp dried	**1 tbsp**
2 tbsp	safflower oil	**2 tbsp**
12.5 cl	dry white wine	**4 fl oz**
2	leeks, trimmed, sliced thickly	**2**

400 g	canned peeled tomatoes, halved, with their liquid	**14 o.**
1 tbsp	fresh rosemary, or ¾ tsp dried	**1 tbs**
6	garlic cloves, finely chopped	**(**
3	bay leaves	**:**
60 cl	unsalted chicken stock	**1 pin**
90 g	dry breadcrumbs	**3 o**
2 tbsp	virgin olive oil	**2 tbs**
2 tsp	chopped fresh parsley	**2 ts**

Place the beans in a saucepan and cover with 5 cm (2 inches) of water. Bring to the boil. Boil for 10 mins, skimming off foam. Reduce the heat. Stir in the pepper and ⅓ of the thyme. Cover and simmer for 35 mins. Drain. Preheat the oven to 190°C (375°F or Mark 5).

In a frying pan, heat the safflower oil over medium-high heat. Add the chicken and brown lightly. Transfer to a plate. Pour off fat and reserve. Pour wine into pan and deglaze over medium-high.

When boiling, add the leeks, tomatoes, rosemary, remaining thyme, salt and ½ the garlic. Simmer, stirring, until tender – about 10 mins.

Spread remaining garlic over the bottom of a casserole. Add half of the beans in an even layer then the chicken, then the bay leaves. Spoon half of the vegetable mixture on top, add remaining beans, then spoon the remaining vegetables over. Pour in 35 cl (12 fl oz) of the stock and sprinkle the breadcrumbs over. Dribble on the reserved fat and olive oil.

Bake for 45 mins. Pour in remaining stock around the edges, without soaking breadcrumbs. Bake for 30 mins or until topping is crunchy and golden and beans are tender. Garnish with parsley.

Jellied Chicken with Lemon and Dill

Serves 8

Working
time: about
30 minutes

Total time:
about 1 day

Calories
340
Protein
43g
Cholesterol
125mg
Total fat
14g
Saturated fat
3g
Sodium
235mg

wo	chickens, skinned, and cut	Two	5 tbsp	chopped fresh dill	5 tbsp
.5 kg	into serving pieces	3 lb	1 litre	unsalted chicken stock	1¾ pints
tsp	salt	¼ tsp	3	large carrots, thinly sliced	3
	freshly ground black pepper		125 g	shelled peas	4 oz
tbsp	virgin olive oil	2 tbsp	8 cl	fresh lemon juice	3 fl oz
	large onion, finely chopped	1			

prinkle the chicken pieces with the salt and epper. Heat the olive oil in a large, heavy frying an and sauté as many pieces as will fit without rowding over medium-high heat until golden – bout 5 minutes on each side. Arrange the ieces in a large casserole.

In the remaining oil, cook the onion over nedium-low heat until translucent – about 0 minutes; stir in half the dill. Spoon the onion nixture on to the chicken pieces. Pour the stock ver all and bring to a simmer on top of the tove. After 20 minutes, turn the pieces, add the arrots and peas, and continue cooking until the

juices run clear when a thigh is pierced with the tip of a sharp knife – about 10 minutes more.

Pour the lemon juice over the chicken and vegetables, and cool to room temperature. Sprinkle the remaining dill on top. Refrigerate for 6 hours or overnight to allow the natural gelatine to set. Serve cold.

Suggested accompaniments: rice salad; sliced tomatoes.

Editor's Note: if fresh dill is unavailable, parsley, tarragon or chervil may be substituted.

Chicken Mole

Serves 6

Working
time: about
1 hour

Total time:
about
2 hours

Calories
295

Protein
28g

Cholesterol
100mg

Total fat
17g

Saturated fat
4g

Sodium
240mg

12	chicken thighs, skinned and boned	**12**
1 tsp	coriander seeds	**1 tsp**
¼ tsp	aniseeds	**¼ tsp**
2	garlic cloves, coarsely chopped	**2**
¼ tsp	cinnamon	**¼ tsp**
¼ tsp	salt	**¼ tsp**
¼ tsp	freshly ground black pepper	**¼ tsp**
2 tbsp	safflower oil	**2 tbsp**
2	hot chili peppers, seeded and chopped	**2**
1	onion, chopped	
2	small ripe tomatoes, skinned, seeded and chopped	
30 cl	unsalted chicken stock	**½ pint**
15 g	plain chocolate, grated	**½ oz**
2 tsp	cornflour, mixed with 2 tbsp red wine	**2 tsp**

In a small pan, toast the coriander and aniseeds over medium heat for 3 to 4 minutes, shaking the pan frequently. Put with the garlic, cinnamon, salt and pepper in a mortar; grind to a paste.

Heat 1 tbsp of the oil in a heavy frying pan over medium heat. Sauté the chilies, stirring constantly until they begin to brown – about 3 mins. Then add the onion, tomatoes and seasoning paste. Cook until almost all the liquid evaporates – about 10 mins. Transfer to a bowl and set aside.

Clean the pan and set it over medium-high heat. Add the remaining tablespoon of oil. Sauté the chicken thighs, in two batches if necessary, so that the pieces do not touch, until they are brown – about 4 mins on each side. Pour off the fat. Add the stock, onion-and-tomato mixture and chocolate. Reduce the heat, cover, and simmer until the juices run clear when a thigh is pierced with a sharp knife – about 20 minutes.

Transfer the pieces to a serving platter and keep them warm. Stir the cornflour-and-wine mixture into the sauce and simmer, stirring frequently, until the sauce is reduced to approximately 35 cl (12 fl oz) – about 7 minutes. Pour the sauce over the chicken.

Curried Chicken with Chutney and Raisins

Serves 4

Working time: about 30 minutes

Total time: about 1 hour

Calories **475**
Protein **45g**
Cholesterol **125mg**
Total fat **22g**
Saturated fat **4g**
Sodium **435mg**

1.5 kg	chicken, skinned, cut into serving pieces	3 lb
½ tsp	salt	½ tsp
½ tsp	freshly ground black pepper	½ tsp
30 g	cornmeal	1 oz
3 tbsps	safflower oil	3 tbsp
1	onion, finely chopped	1
1	carrot, finely chopped	1
½	small green pepper, finely chopped	½
3	garlic cloves, finely chopped	3
350 g	tomatoes, preferably the Italian plum, skinned, seeded and coarsely chopped, with juice reserved	12 oz
35 cl	unsalted chicken stock	12 fl oz
1 tbsp	curry powder	1 tbsp
2 tsp	mango chutney	2 tsp
1	bay leaf	1
1½ tbsp	raisins	1½ tbsp
1½ tbsp	sultanas	1½ tbsp
1 tbsp	sesame seeds	1 tbsp

Sprinkle the chicken with seasoning, and dredge lightly in the cornmeal. In a casserole large enough to hold the chicken in a single layer, heat 2 tbsps oil over medium heat. Brown the chicken for 2 mins on each side. Remove it and set it aside. Preheat the oven to 180°C (350°F or Mark 4).

Put the remaining oil into the casserole. Add onion, carrot and green pepper, sauté lightly for 1 min. Add garlic and sauté for 30 secs more. Pour in the tomatoes, their juice and the stock. Stir in curry powder, chutney, bay leaf, and 1 tbsp each of raisins and sultanas. Return chicken

to the casserole and bring to a simmer. Bake, covered, for 10 mins. At the same time, brown the sesame seeds in a pie tin in the oven.

When the breasts feel firm but springy, remove them from the oven and set them aside, covered with foil, on a plate, leaving the other chicken pieces in the casserole. Bake the other pieces until the juices run clear when a thigh is pierced with a sharp knife – about 5 mins more. Serve the chicken with the toasted sesame seeds and the remaining raisins and sultanas scattered across the top.

Chicken with Dark Rum, Papaya, Mango and Banan

Serves 4

Working time: about 30 minutes

Total time: about 50 minutes

Calories 540

Protein 30g

Cholesterol 110mg

Total fat 18g

Saturated fat 6g

Sodium 395mg

4	whole chicken legs, skinned, cut into thighs and drumsticks	4
½ tsp	salt	½ tsp
	freshly ground white pepper	
1 tbsp	safflower oil	1 tbsp
1	large onion, cut into eighths, layers separated	1
2	garlic cloves, finely chopped	2
2 tsp	finely chopped fresh ginger root	2 tsp
¼ litre	dark rum	8 fl oz
½ litre	unsalted chicken stock	16 fl oz
4 tbsp	double cream	4 tbsp
1	large tomato, skinned, cored, seeded and cut into large chunks	
1	medium papaya, scooped into balls with a melon-baller or cut into cubes, extra flesh chopped and reserved	
1	small mango, peeled and cut into cubes	
1	small banana, cut into 1 cm (½ inch) slices	
⅛ tsp	freshly grated nutmeg	⅛ tsp

Sprinkle the chicken with ¼ teaspoon of the salt and some pepper. In a large casserole, heat the oil over medium heat. Brown the chicken pieces lightly – about 4 minutes on each side.

Add the onion and cook, stirring, until it is translucent – about 5 mins. Add garlic and ginger, cook for 1 min more. Remove from heat and cool for 1 min. Reserve 1 tsp of the rum, pour the rest into the casserole. Return to heat, simmer until reduced by half – about 5 mins.

Add stock and bring to boil. Reduce heat, simmer until juices run clear when a thigh is pierced with a knife – about 5 minutes more. Transfer chicken to a platter and cover with foil.

In a pan, bring the cream, tomato and extra papaya flesh to a simmer. Pour in the braising liquid and simmer until the sauce thickens slightly – about 3 minutes. Purée the mixture in a processor or blender, and return it to the pan.

Add the papaya, mango, banana, nutmeg, reserved teaspoon of rum and remaining salt, cook just until the fruit is heated through – about 1 minute. Remove foil and pour over sauce. Serve immediately.

Chicken Drumsticks Cacciatore

Serves 6

Working time: about 40 minutes

Total time: about 1 hour and 30 minutes

Calories 305

Protein 30g

Cholesterol 95mg

Total fat 14g

Saturated fat 3g

Sodium 365mg

12	chicken drumsticks	**12**	
¼ tsp	salt	**¼ tsp**	
	freshly ground black pepper		
1 tbsp	virgin olive oil	**1 tbsp**	
1	onion, finely chopped	**1**	
1	small carrot, thinly sliced	**1**	
1	small stick celery, thinly sliced	**1**	
1	large green pepper, seeded, deribbed and diced	**1**	
1	small sweet red pepper, seeded, deribbed and diced	**1**	
5	garlic cloves, finely chopped	**5**	
2 tsp	fresh oregano leaves, chopped or ¾ tsp dried oregano	**2 tsp**	
1 tsp	fresh thyme, or ¼ tsp dried thyme	**1 tsp**	
800 g	canned plum tomatoes, drained and chopped, with the juice reserved	**1lb 12 oz**	
12.5 cl	dry white wine	**4 fl oz**	
2 tbsp	chopped parsley	**2 tbsp**	

Rub the chicken with half the salt and the pepper. In a casserole, heat the oil over medium-high heat. Add drumsticks and brown – about 12 minutes. Transfer the pieces to a plate.

Reduce the heat to medium. Combine the onion, carrot, celery, green and red peppers, and garlic in the casserole. Sprinkle the oregano and thyme over the vegetables and stir. Sauté until the peppers are softened – about 5 minutes. Preheat the oven to 170°C (325°F or Mark 3).

Add the tomato to the casserole and raise the heat, stirring until the excess liquid evaporates

– about 7 mins. Pour in the wine and reserved tomato juice. Simmer until reduced by ⅓ – about 10 mins. Immerse the drumsticks in the sauce. Season with remaining salt and some pepper.

Cover the casserole and braise the chicken in the oven until the meat is tender and clings loosely to the bone – about 30 mins. Place it in a serving dish.

Place the uncovered casserole over high heat. Add the parsley, then reduce the sauce by ⅓ – about 5 mins. Spoon sauce over the drumsticks and serve.

Chicken Legs Stewed with Prunes

Serves 4

Working time: about 40 minutes

Total time: about 3 hours and 45 minutes

Calories 500

Protein 30g

Cholesterol 100mg

Total fat 12g

Saturated fat 4g

Sodium 265mg

4	large chicken legs, skinned	**4**
¼ litre	brandy	**8 fl oz**
20	stoned prunes (about 150 g/5 oz)	**20**
15 g	unsalted butter	**½ oz**
¼ tsp	salt	**¼ tsp**
	freshly ground white pepper	
1	large onion, cut in half, thinly sliced	**1**
1	large carrot, cut diagonally into 5 mm (¼ inch) slices	**1**
4	garlic cloves, finely chopped	
1 tsp	dry mustard	**1 tsp**
1 tsp	fresh thyme, or ¼ tsp dried thyme	**1 tsp**
40 cl	unsalted chicken stock	**14 fl oz**
10	parsley stems, tied in a bunch with string	**10**
3 tbsp	fresh lemon juice	**3 tbsp**
1 tbsp	chopped fresh parsley	**1 tbsp**

Pour brandy over the prunes and marinate for at least 2 hours at room temperature, or alternatively leave them to stand overnight in the refrigerator.

Heat the butter in a frying pan over medium-high. Lightly brown the chicken for about 5 minutes on each side. Sprinkle the salt and pepper over the legs and transfer to a large, casserole, set them aside. In the pan used to brown the legs, combine onion, carrot, garlic, mustard and thyme, and reduce heat to medium. Sauté, stirring frequently, until the onion is translucent – 5 to 7 minutes.

Preheat the oven to 170°C (325°F or Mark 3).

Add the prunes, brandy and stock to the onion-and-carrot mixture. Simmer and continue cooking for 3 minutes, then empty the pan into the casserole; the mixture should nearly cover the legs. Drop in the bunch of parsley stalks.

Cover and cook in the oven for 1 hour Reduce the oven temperature to 100°C (200°F or Mark ¼). Transfer the legs to a platter and cover with foil. Add the lemon juice to the sauce remove the bunch of parsley and reduce the liquid by half over medium heat – 15 to 20 minutes. Pour sauce over the legs and serve immediately, garnished with chopped parsley

Lemon-Mustard Chicken with Root Vegetables

Serves 6

Working time: about 20 minutes

Total time: about 45 minutes

Calories 265

Protein 29g

Cholesterol 80mg

Total fat 9g

Saturated fat 3g

Sodium 260mg

	large chicken breasts, skinned, fat removed	6
tbsp	safflower oil	**1 tbsp**
0 g	unsalted butter	**1 oz**
	onion, cut into 12 pieces	1
	garlic clove, finely chopped	1
2.5 cl	dry sherry	**4 fl oz**
tsp	salt	**¼ tsp**
	freshly ground black pepper	

2 tbsp	fresh lemon juice	**2 tbsp**
2 tbsp	Dijon mustard	**2 tbsp**
½ litre	unsalted chicken stock	**16 fl oz**
2	carrots, cut into 1 cm (½ inch) rounds	2
2	parsnips, cut into 1 cm (½ inch) rounds	2
1	small swede, or 2 medium turnips, cut into 1 cm (½ inch) cubes	1
1	lemon, grated rind only	1
4 tbsp	chopped parsley	**4 tbsp**

Heat the oil and butter in a large, heavy frying pan or fireproof casserole over medium-high heat. Sauté the chicken, bone side up, until the pieces turn golden – about 4 minutes. Remove the chicken and set it aside. Add the onion pieces to the pan, and sauté for 2 minutes. Add the garlic and sauté for about 15 seconds. Pour off the fat. Add the sherry to deglaze the pan, and stir. Lower the heat and simmer until the liquid is reduced by half – about 4 minutes.

Return the chicken breasts, bone side down, to the simmering mixture and sprinkle them with the salt and pepper. Stir in the lemon juice, mustard and stock; then add the carrots, parsnips and swede or turnips. Bring the sauce to the boil, stirring. Reduce the heat to low, partially cover the pan, and simmer until the vegetables are tender – about 20 minutes. Arrange the chicken and vegetables in a serving dish. Pour the sauce over the chicken, and garnish with the lemon and parsley before serving.

Suggested accompaniments: curly endive salad; dark rye bread.

Braised Chicken, Almonds and Chick-Peas

Serves 4

Working time: about 20 minutes

Total time: about 1 day

Calories 680

Protein 51g

Cholesterol 105mg

Total fat 25g

Saturated fat 4g

Sodium 615mg

1.25 kg	chicken, skinned and cut into quarters	**2½ lb**
200 g	dried chick-peas, soaked overnight in water and drained	**7 oz**
75 g	blanched almonds, toasted and coarsely chopped	**2½ oz**
1 tsp	wholemeal flour	**1 tsp**
¼ tsp	salt	**¼ tsp**
¼ tsp	freshly ground black pepper	**¼ tsp**
2 tbsp	virgin olive oil	**2 tbsp**

1	large onion, chopped	**1**
4	garlic cloves, finely chopped	**4**
½ tsp	ground ginger	**½ tsp**
⅛ tsp	ground turmeric	**⅛ tsp**
⅛ tsp	ground cinnamon	**⅛ tsp**
⅛ tsp	ground cumin	**⅛ tsp**
2 tbsp	currants	**2 tbsp**
60 cl	unsalted chicken stock	**1 pint**
2 tbsp	fresh lemon juice	**2 tbsp**
200 g	couscous	**7 oz**

Put the chick-peas in a pan, covering with water to a level 2.5 cm (1 inch) above them. Bring to the boil, then simmer for 1 hour. Drain and place in a casserole with the almonds.

Preheat the oven to 180°C (350°F or Mark 4). Mix the flour with the seasoning, dust the chicken all over. Sauté in olive oil over medium-high heat until browned – 5 mins each side. Place on top of the chick-peas and almonds.

In the sauté pan, cook the onion until translucent – 10 mins. Add the garlic, spices and currants, mix well. Cook another 2 to 3 minutes. Spoon the mixture on to chicken.

Add ¼ litre (8 fl oz) of stock and the lemon juice and bring to a simmer; cover and place it in the oven. Cook until chicken juices run clear when a thigh is pierced with a sharp knife – 45 mins.

Shortly before the chicken is done, bring the remaining stock to the boil in a pan and slowly pour in the couscous, stirring. Remove from heat and stand 5 minutes, then fluff with a fork.

Spoon the couscous on to a serving platter and arrange the chicken pieces, chick-peas and almonds on top. Pour the juices over all.

Chicken Casserole with Dried Fruits and Onions

Serves 4

Working time: about 30 minutes

Total time: about 1 hour and 45 minutes

Calories 585

Protein 34g

Cholesterol 110mg

Total fat 20g

Saturated fat 6g

Sodium 470mg

	chicken thighs, skinned	8	45 g	dried apricots, cut in half	1½ oz
tbsp	safflower oil	1 tbsp	45 g	sultanas	1½ oz
5 g	unsalted butter, plus ½ tsp	½ oz	45 g	currants	1½ oz
tsp	salt	½ tsp	1 tbsp	grainy mustard	1 tbsp
	freshly ground black pepper		¼ tsp	grated orange rind (optional)	¼ tsp
75 g	long-grain brown rice	6 oz	125 g	pearl onions, blanched, peeled	4 oz
	small onion, chopped	1	⅛ tsp	sugar	⅛ tsp
0 cl	unsalted chicken stock	1 pint			
	bouquet garni; 2 sprigs thyme, parsley 1 bunch, 1 bay leaf	1			

n a large casserole, heat the oil and the 15 g ½ oz) butter over medium-high. Cook chicken highs, 4 at a time, on one side until lightly rowned – 4 mins. Turn and sprinkle with teaspoon salt and some pepper. Sauté on the econd side for 3 mins. Remove from the casserole nd set aside.

Reduce heat. Add rice and onion, cook until rains are translucent – 5 mins. Add 35 cl (12 fl oz) f stock, remaining salt and bouquet garni. Bring o boil. Cover, simmer for 20 minutes. Preheat he oven to 180°C (350°F or Mark 4).

Stir the fruit, mustard and orange rind, into the casserole. Return the chicken to the casserole, pressing it into the rice. Pour on the remaining stock. Cover and bake for 35 mins.

Put onions in a pan with the sugar and the ½ tsp butter. Cover with water. Boil until no water remains – 10 to 15 mins. Watching lest the onions burn, shake the pan until they are evenly browned. Add the onions to the casserole and bake until rice is tender – 15 mins. Remove the bouquet garni and serve the casserole.

Chicken Fricassee with Watercress

Serves 4

Working time: about 45 minutes

Total time: about 45 minutes

Calories 250
Protein 18g
Cholesterol 60mg
Total fat 10g
Saturated fat 4g
Sodium 250mg

4	large chicken thighs, skinned, boned, excess fat removed, meat cut into 2.5 cm (1 inch) cubes	4
12.5 cl	plain low-fat yogurt	4 fl oz
2 tbsp	single cream	2 tbsp
2 tbsp	cornflour, mixed with 4 tbsp water	2 tbsp
2 tsp	fresh thyme, or ½ tsp dried thyme	2 tsp
1 tsp	fresh rosemary, or ¼ tsp dried rosemary	1 tsp
15 g	unsalted butter	½ oz
2	carrots, julienned	2
250 g	mushrooms, thickly sliced	8 oz
3 tbsp	finely chopped shallots	3 tbsp
½ tsp	ground cumin	½ tsp
12.5 cl	dry white wine	4 fl oz
12.5 cl	unsalted chicken stock	4 fl oz
4	garlic cloves, finely chopped	4
¼ tsp	salt	¼ tsp
2	bunches watercress, thick stems removed	2

In a bowl, combine the yogurt, cream, cornflour mixture, thyme and rosemary. Set aside.

Melt the butter over medium heat in a large, heavy frying pan. Add the carrots and cook for 2 minutes, stirring once. Stir in the chicken, mushrooms, shallots, wine, stock, garlic, salt and the yogurt mixture. Reduce the heat to medium low, cover, and cook for 5 minutes.

Uncover and stir well. Scatter the watercress over the top but do not stir it in; it should be allowed to steam. Cover again and cook until the chicken is done – about 5 minutes more.

Drain the contents in a colander, catching the sauce in a bowl. Put the contents of the colander on a platter and set aside to keep warm.

Return the sauce to the pan. Over medium heat, whisking occasionally to keep the sauce from burning, reduce it by approximately half. This should take 10 to 15 minutes. Return the chicken mixture to the pan, and stir to coat the chicken with the sauce. Serve at once.

Suggested accompaniment: pasta with tomato and Parmesan cheese.

Braised Chicken with Potatoes, Leeks and Kale

Serves 4

Working time: about 30 minutes

Total time: about 1 hour and 15 minutes

Calories 440

Protein 42g

Cholesterol 125mg

Total fat 23g

Saturated fat 6g

Sodium 540mg

.75 kg	chicken	3½ lb
	freshly ground black pepper	
tsp	salt	¾ tsp
tbsp	safflower oil	1 tbsp
	leek, halved lengthwise, cleaned thoroughly and cut into 1 cm (½ inch) slices	1
2 tbsp	thinly sliced shallots	2 tbsp
125 g	fresh kale, stemmed, washed and coarsely chopped	4 oz
2 tsp	fresh thyme, or ½ tsp dried thyme	2 tsp
½ tsp	cayenne pepper	½ tsp
3	red potatoes, unpeeled, cut into 4 cm (1½ inch) pieces	3

Rub the inside of the chicken with pepper and ¾ teaspoon of the salt, and truss the bird.

In a large, fireproof casserole, heat the oil over medium-high heat. Add the leek, shallots and kale, and sauté until the kale begins to wilt. Pour in 1 litre (1¾ pints) of water, then add the remaining salt, some more pepper and the thyme. Place the chicken in the casserole and sprinkle the cayenne pepper over it. Bring the liquid to the boil, reduce the heat to low, partially cover and simmer for 50 minutes.

Transfer the chicken from the casserole to a warmed platter. Cover it with foil to keep it warm. Skim off any fat in the casserole. Add the potatoes and simmer until they are tender – about 10 minutes. Arrange the vegetables round the chicken and pour the braising liquid over it.

Chicken Rolled in Vine Leaves

Serves 4

Working time: about 30 minutes

Total time: about 1 day

Calories 465

Protein 36g

Cholesterol 60mg

Total fat 19g

Saturated fat 4g

Sodium 550mg

350 g	chicken breast meat, cut into 1 cm ($\frac{1}{2}$ inch) cubes	**12 oz**
$\frac{1}{2}$ litre	unsalted chicken stock	**16 fl oz**
250 g	yellow split peas, soaked overnight and drained	**8 oz**
1 tsp	chopped fresh mint	**1 tsp**
2 tbsp	chopped fresh coriander	**2 tbsp**
$\frac{3}{4}$ tsp	salt	**$\frac{3}{4}$ tsp**
	freshly ground black pepper	

1	medium aubergine, peeled, cubed	
2 tbsp	safflower oil	**2 tbsp**
5	garlic cloves, peeled and bruised	
2 tbsp	tahini	**2 tbsp**
4	black olives, stoned	
2 tsp	fresh lemon juice	**2 tsp**
8	vine leaves, preserved in brine	
4	tomatoes, halved	
15 g	unsalted butter, melted	**$\frac{1}{2}$ oz**

Put the stock, peas, mint, $\frac{1}{2}$ the coriander, $\frac{1}{4}$ tsp salt and some pepper in a pan and boil. Cover, simmer until peas are cooked – 45 minutes.

Toss the aubergine cubes with $\frac{1}{4}$ teaspoon of the salt and drain them on paper towels.

Season the chicken with remaining $\frac{1}{4}$ salt and some pepper. Heat 1 tbsp oil in a frying pan over medium-high. Sauté the chicken until browned – 4 mins. Transfer to a bowl.

Add remaining oil to the pan and sauté the garlic for 2 minutes. Transfer to a' processor. Sauté the aubergine in the oil remaining in the pan until brown – 5 mins. Add aubergine, tahini,

remaining coriander, olives, lemon juice and some pepper to the processor, and purée. Reserve 2 tbsps for garnish and mix remaining purée with chicken. Preheat the oven to 180°C (350°F or Mark 4).

Rinse the vine leaves and lay them flat. Place 2 tbsps chicken mixture on each. Fold the sides of each leaf in to encase the filling, and roll it up. Spread the peas in a baking dish and place the rolled vine leaves on top. Arrange tomato halves in between, topped with reserved filling. Bake for 15 mins. Serve, brushed with melted butter.

Plum-Coated Chicken with Chinese Cabbage

Serves 8

Working time: about 1 hour and 30 minutes

Total time: about 2 hours

Calories 270

Protein 23g

Cholesterol 70mg

Total fat 13g

Saturated fat 4g

Sodium 315mg

Kg	chicken pieces, skinned	6 lb	30 g	unsalted butter	1 oz
	Chinese cabbages (750 g/1½ lb)	2	2 tbsp	fresh lemon juice	2 tbsp
litre	unsalted chicken stock	1¾ pints	1 tbsp	safflower oil	1 tbsp
	large ripe red plums	5	¾ tsp	salt	¾ tsp
tbsp	honey	2 tbsp	1 tbsp	virgin olive oil	1 tbsp
2.5 cl	red wine vinegar	4 fl oz			

im cabbages; rinse leaves and pat dry. Discard
e white core at leaf bases. Slice leaves into 5 cm
inch) squares and set aside.

Bring stock to the boil. Cut a cross on the
ottom of each plum, boil the plums in the stock
til the skin begins to peel – 2 mins. Peel plums
d set aside. Stir 1 tbsp honey and ½ the vinegar
to stock. Reduce liquid to half and set it aside.

Meanwhile, cut the plums in half, remove
ones and cut into cubes. Melt the butter in a pan
er medium heat. Add the plums, remaining
oney and vinegar. Cook, stirring, until the
ums are reduced to a dense, pasty consistency
45 to 60 mins. Stir in 12.5 cl (4 fl oz) of the stock
d the lemon juice. Transfer to a blender.
ocess until smooth.

Simmer remaining stock to reduce to about

17.5 cl (6 fl oz). Strain, set aside.

While the stock is simmering, heat the safflower
oil over medium-high. Sauté the chicken on one
side until brown. Turn, sprinkle with ¼ tsp of the
salt, cook on second side till brown – 3 to 4 mins.
Reserve pan for the cabbage. Preheat the oven to
200°C (400°F or Mark 6).

Arrange the chicken, in a dish. Brush a thick
coat of plum sauce over each. Whisk remaining
sauce into reduced stock. Bake chicken until the
juices run clear – 30 mins.

While chicken is cooking, steam the cabbage
until wilted. Heat olive oil in a pan and toss in the
cabbage to coat it.

Place cabbage under cooked chicken. Warm
the sauce and spoon it over.

47

Honey-Basil Chicken

Serves 4

Working time: about 20 minutes

Total time: about 1 hour

Calories
260

Protein
27g

Cholesterol
90mg

Total fat
12g

Saturated fat
3g

Sodium
215mg

4	whole chicken legs, skinned	4	2 tbsp	honey	2 tbsp
$\frac{1}{4}$ tsp	salt	$\frac{1}{4}$ tsp	2 tbsp	unsalted chicken stock	2 tbsp
	freshly ground black pepper		2	garlic cloves, thinly sliced	
1 tbsp	safflower oil	1 tbsp	30–40	fresh basil leaves	30–40
7.5 g	unsalted butter	$\frac{1}{4}$ oz			

Preheat the oven to 200°C (400°F or Mark 6). Cut a piece of aluminium foil 30 cm (1 ft) square for each leg. Sprinkle the legs with the salt and pepper. Heat the oil and butter in a frying pan over medium heat, then brown the legs for about 2 minutes on each side. Put a leg in the middle of each foil square, and dribble $1\frac{1}{2}$ teaspoons of the honey and $1\frac{1}{2}$ teaspoons of the stock over each one. Lay one quarter of the garlic slices on each piece, cover with a loose layer of the basil leaves, and wrap the foil snugly over the top. Put the foil packages on a baking sheet and set it in the oven.

After 30 minutes, remove a foil package from the oven and unwrap it carefully to preserve the juices. Test for doneness by piercing the thigh with the tip of a sharp knife; if the juices run clear, it is done. If necessary, return the leg to the oven and bake about 5 minutes more.

To serve, undo each package and transfer the legs to a platter. Remove any garlic or basil that sticks to the foil and put them back on the chicken. Pour the collected juices from the foil packages over the legs.

Suggested accompaniments: steamed carrot, cos lettuce salad.

Baked Chicken Breasts Stuffed with Tahini

Serves 4

Working time: about 30 minutes

Total time: about 45 minutes

Calories 360
Protein 32g
Cholesterol 75mg
Total fat 17g
Saturated fat 3g
Sodium 455mg

4	chicken breasts, skinned and boned	4
2 tbsp	tahini, or 2 tbsp toasted sesame seeds pulverized with a mortar and pestle	2 tbsp
2 tbsp	chopped parsley	2 tbsp
2	garlic cloves, finely chopped	2
1 tsp	fresh lemon juice	1 tsp
⅛ tsp	cayenne pepper	⅛ tsp
½ tsp	salt	½ tsp
	freshly ground black pepper	

2 tbsp	plain low-fat yogurt	2 tbsp
2 tbsp	sesame seeds	2 tbsp
45 g	dry breadcrumbs	1½ oz
1½ tbsp	safflower oil	1½ tbsp
1	shallot, thinly sliced	1
4 tbsp	sherry	4 tbsp
¼ litre	unsalted chicken stock	8 fl oz
2 tsp	cornflour, mixed with 1 tbsp water	2 tsp
1	tomato, skinned, seeded and cut into strips	1

To make the stuffing, combine the tahini, parsley, garlic, lemon juice and cayenne in a bowl. Cut a pocket horizontally in each breast half. Stuff one quarter of the tahini and herb mixture into each breast pocket. Sprinkle the chicken with ¼ teaspoon of the salt and some pepper.

Preheat the oven to 180°C (350°F or Mark 4). To breadcrumb the pieces, first coat with yogurt. Mix the sesame seeds with the breadcrumbs, and coat the breasts in this mixture. Heat 1 tbsp oil in a casserole over medium heat. Cook chicken until golden-brown – about 3 minutes per side.

Place the casserole in the oven and bake, turning once, until chicken feels firm but springy to the touch – about 15 minutes. Transfer chicken to a serving platter and keep it warm.

For the sauce, heat remaining oil in a small pan over medium-high. Sauté the shallot for 1 min, add the sherry and reduce to about 1 tbsp. Add the stock and bring to a simmer. Stir in the cornflour mixture and cook 2 mins more. Stir in the tomato strips, and season. Pour the sauce over the chicken breasts and serve.

Baked Chicken Legs Stuffed with Millet

Serves 4

Working time: about 45 minutes

Total time: about 2 hours

Calories 405

Protein 36g

Cholesterol 125mg

Total fat 24g

Saturated fat 8g

Sodium 345mg

4	chicken legs	4	⅛ tsp	salt	⅛ tsp
15 g	unsalted butter	½ oz		freshly ground black pepper	
1	onion, chopped	1	30 g	prosciutto, cut into thin strips	1 oz
4 tbsp	millet	4 tbsp	60 g	low-fat mozzarella, diced	2 oz
½ tsp	fresh rosemary, or ⅛ tsp dried	½ tsp	2 tsp	safflower oil	2 tsp
¾ tsp	chopped fresh sage, or ⅛ tsp dried	¾ tsp	2 tbsp	dry white wine	2 tbsp
12.5 cl	unsalted chicken stock	4 fl oz			

Heat the butter over medium-low heat in a small, heavy-bottomed saucepan. Add the onion and cook until translucent – about 5 mins. Add the millet and herbs, and cook for 4 mins. Stir in the stock, salt and pepper, and bring to the boil. Reduce the heat to low, cover, simmer until the liquid is gone – about 20 mins. The millet should be tender but not mushy. Empty into a bowl and cool before stirring in the prosciutto and mozzarella.

Meanwhile, place the legs skin side down on a work surface. Remove the thigh bone from each leg: beginning at the end of the bone, gently scrape and cut the flesh away with the tip of a small, sharp knife, until you reach the joint. Prise the bone away from the joint and remove the bone. To make a pocket for

the stuffing, start a cut at the channel left by the bone and work outwards towards the edge of the thigh, stopping just short of slicing through to the skin. Repeat the process on the other side of the channel.

Mound stuffing on to the centre of each thigh. Close the meat back over, wrapping the skin over the openings. Mould each into a log shape and sew it up with a needle and thick thread. Preheat the oven to 180°C (350°F or Mark 4).

Heat the oil in a frying pan over medium-high. Sauté the legs, until they turn golden. Transfer to a dish. Discard the fat and deglaze the pan with the wine; pour the liquid over the chicken. Bake until the legs are cooked – about 20 minutes. Serve immediately.

Chicken Pillows

Serves 6

Working time: about 1 hour

Total time: about 1 hour and 30 minutes

Calories 350

Protein 34g

Cholesterol 80mg

Total fat 16g

Saturated fat 4g

Sodium 350mg

	chicken breasts, skinned, boned, long triangular fillets removed and reserved for another use, lightly pounded	**6**
tbsp	fresh lemon juice	**2 tbsp**
tbsp	virgin olive oil	**3 tbsp**
0 g	low-fat mozzarella, cut into 6 slices	**3 oz**
	carrots, cut into 5 mm (¼ inch) by 12.5 cm (5 inches) strips, blanched for 3 mins	**2**
	courgette, cut into 5 mm (¼ inch) by 12.5 cm (5 inches) strips, blanched for 30 secs	**1**
	spring onions, trimmed to 12.5 cm (5 inches) in length, blanched for 1 min	**6**

30 g	fresh breadcrumbs	**1 oz**
1	garlic clove, finely chopped	**1**
⅛ tsp	salt	**⅛ tsp**
2 tbsp	finely chopped fresh mixed herbs	**2 tbsp**
	Tomato-Garlic Sauce	
3	ripe tomatoes, skinned, seeded and coarsely chopped	**3**
2	garlic cloves, finely chopped	**2**
2	spring onions, finely chopped	**2**
1 tbsp	virgin olive oil	**1 tbsp**
¼ tsp	salt	**¼ tsp**
	freshly ground black pepper	
4 tbsp	finely chopped basil or parsley	**4 tbsp**

Marinate the chicken in the lemon juice and 1 tbsp oil for 1 hour, turning occasionally.

Prepare the sauce. In a pan, mix the tomatoes, garlic, spring onions, oil, salt and pepper. Bring to the boil, reduce heat, simmer until it thickens – 10 mins. Remove from heat and add basil. Preheat the oven to 190°C (375°F or Mark 5).

Remove breasts from the marinade and place smooth side down. Reserve the marinade. Lay a slice of the mozzarella on each. Put 1 strip of each vegetable across top. Roll up breasts and secure with wooden picks. Arrange in a baking dish. Brush with marinade and cover with foil. Bake (20 mins).

Heat remaining oil and gently brown the breadcrumbs. Add the garlic, salt and herbs.

Sprinkle breadcrumb mixture on cooked chicken. Grill until golden. Remove picks, arrange on a platter, and serve with re-heated tomato sauce.

Spicy Yogurt-Baked Chicken Thighs

Serves 4

Working time: about 25 minutes

Total time: about 2 hours and 30 minutes

Calories 275

Protein 31g

Cholesterol 100mg

Total fat 13g

Saturated fat 4g

Sodium 135mg

8	chicken thighs, skinned, fat removed	**8**
¼ litre	plain low-fat yogurt	**8 fl oz**
2 tbsp	fresh lime juice	**2 tbsp**
2 tsp	grated fresh ginger root	**2 tsp**
4	garlic cloves, finely chopped	**4**
1 tsp	ground cumin	**1 tsp**
1 tsp	turmeric	**1 tsp**
½ tsp	cayenne pepper	**½ ts**
1 tsp	aniseeds or fennel seeds, ground coarsely in a mortar and pestle	**1 ts**
1 tsp	cornflour, mixed with 2 tsp water	**1 ts**
1	lime, cut into slices, for garnish	

To prepare the marinade, combine the yogurt, lime juice, ginger, garlic and spices in a bowl and mix well. Place the chicken thighs in the marinade and stir to coat them. Cover the bowl and refrigerate it for 2 to 8 hours. (The yogurt will tenderize as well as flavour the meat.) Preheat the oven to 180°C (350°F or Mark 4).

Arrange the thighs in a large, shallow baking dish, leaving no more than 2.5 cm (1 inch) of space between them; reserve the marinade.

Bake for 10 minutes. Stir the cornflour mixtur into the marinade, then spread the mixture ove the chicken pieces. Bake until the meat fee firm but springy to the touch – 10 to 15 minute more. Transfer to a serving platter, arrange th lime slices around the thighs, and serve.

Suggested accompaniments: rice with raisin: chutney.

Spinach-Stuffed Chicken Breasts

Serves 4

Working time: about 5 minutes

Total time: about 1 hour

Calories 430

Protein 44g

Cholesterol 110mg

Total fat 22g

Saturated fat 9g

Sodium 685mg

chicken breasts, boned, skin left on (about 500 g/1 lb)		4
fresh thyme, or ¼ tsp dried thyme		1 tsp
salt		¼ tsp
virgin olive oil		1 tsp
Spinach and Cheese Stuffing		
onion, finely chopped		1
unsalted butter		½ oz
virgin olive oil		1 tbsp
spinach, washed, stemmed and coarsely chopped		1 lb
low-fat ricotta cheese		4 oz
Parmesan cheese, freshly grated	60 g	2 oz
finely chopped fresh basil, or ½ tsp dried basil	1 tsp	1 tsp
freshly ground black pepper		
Yogurt-Tomato Sauce		
plain low-fat yogurt	¼ litre	8 fl oz
red wine vinegar	1 tbsp	1 tbsp
salt	¼ tsp	¼ tsp
ripe tomato, skinned, seeded and finely chopped	1	1
large basil leaves, thinly sliced	4	4
freshly ground black pepper		

the stuffing, cook the onion in the fats in a ing pan until translucent. Add spinach and ok until wilted and moisture has evaporated bout 6 mins. Transfer to a bowl and cool. Stir the cheeses, basil and some pepper.

To make the sauce, mix the yogurt, vinegar d salt. Reserve 1 tsp of the tomato and 1 tsp of sil, stir the rest into the yogurt. Add pepper to te. Transfer sauce to a serving bowl, garnish with reserved tomato and basil, set aside. eheat the oven to 190°C (375°F or Mark 5).

Make pockets for the stuffing by running a finger between the flesh and skin on one long side of each breast. Rub the thyme and salt into the flesh. Dribble ¼ tsp of olive oil on to the skin of each. Fill each pocket with ¼ of the stuffing. Place skin side up in an oiled dish, and bake until skin turns golden-brown – about 25 minutes.

Remove from the oven. Allow to cool for a few minutes. Cut each into 1 cm (½ inch) wide slices and arrange on a warmed platter or on individual plates. Serve with the yogurt sauce.

Cajun Chicken Wings

Serves 4

Working time: about 20 minutes

Total time: about 1 hour

Calories 335
Protein 28g
Cholesterol 85mg
Total fat 21g
Saturated fat 6g
Sodium 355mg

12	chicken wings, tips removed	12
5	dried bay leaves, crumbled into small bits	5
$\frac{3}{4}$ tsp	caraway seeds	$\frac{3}{4}$ tsp
$\frac{1}{2}$ to $\frac{3}{4}$ tsp	cayenne pepper	$\frac{1}{2}$ to $\frac{3}{4}$ tsp
$\frac{3}{4}$ tsp	ground coriander	$\frac{3}{4}$ tsp
$\frac{3}{4}$ tsp	ground cumin	$\frac{3}{4}$ tsp
4	garlic cloves, finely chopped	
$1\frac{1}{2}$ tsp	dry mustard	$1\frac{1}{2}$ tsp
2 tsp	paprika	2 tsp
$\frac{3}{4}$ tsp	dried thyme	$\frac{3}{4}$ tsp
$\frac{1}{2}$ tsp	salt	$\frac{1}{2}$ tsp
2 tbsp	brandy	2 tbsp
2 tbsp	fresh lemon or lime juice	2 tbsp

Defat the chicken wings by cooking them in boiling water for 10 minutes. Drain, and set aside to cool. Preheat the oven to 190°C (375°F or Mark 5).

Using a large mortar and pestle, grind the bay leaf bits to a fine powder, then add the caraway seeds, cayenne pepper, coriander, cumin, garlic, mustard, paprika, thyme and salt and grind together for about 10 minutes. Add the brandy and lemon or lime juice to the pulverized herbs and stir into a thick paste.

With a pastry brush, cover both sides of each wing with the herb paste. When no more paste remains in the mortar, squeeze the last few drops from the brush. Arrange the chicken wings on a baking sheet.

Bake until the skin turns a deep brown and is quite crisp – 30 to 35 minutes.

Suggested accompaniments: steamed vegetable marrow; sautéed mushrooms.

Chicken Wrapped in Crisp Phyllo

Serves 6

Working time: about 1 hour

Total time: about 1 day

Calories 500

Protein 37g

Cholesterol 95mg

Total fat 27g

Saturated fat 7g

Sodium 545mg

6	chicken breasts, skinned and boned (about 750 g/1½ lb)	6
250 g	phyllo pastry (18 sheets)	8 oz
¾ tsp	salt	¾ tsp
¾ tsp	freshly ground black pepper	¾ tsp
4 tbsp	safflower oil	4 tbsp
1	garlic clove, finely chopped	1
1	shallot, finely chopped	1
350 g	fresh spinach, washed and stemmed	12 oz
4 tbsp	dry white wine	4 tbsp
¼ litre	unsalted chicken stock	8 fl oz
1 tbsp	double cream	1 tbsp
60 g	pistachio nuts, shelled, peeled and coarsely chopped	2 oz
250 g	low-fat ricotta cheese	8 oz

Slice each breast diagonally into three medallions. Sprinkle with ½ tsp of salt and pepper. Heat 1 tbsp oil in a frying pan. Sear the pieces for about 30 secs on each side in batches, adding 2 tbsps oil as necessary. Set aside on a plate.

Add garlic and shallot to pan, sauté for about 30 secs, stirring. Add spinach, reduce heat to low, and cover. Cook until spinach is wilted – about 2 mins. Remove from heat and take out ½ of mixture. Chop finely and reserve for filling.

Heat pan again over medium heat. Add wine and stock, stir to deglaze. Stir in remaining salt, pepper and cream, cook until reduced by half. Purée in a blender. Pour into a pan, set aside. Preheat the oven to 170°C (325°F or Mark 3).

To make filling, mix the pistachios, ricotta and chopped spinach mixture. Blot the medallions dry. Place three phyllo sheets, stacked, on work surface. Cover remaining sheets with a damp paper towel. Centre a piece of chicken near an edge of the phyllo. Spread with a thin layer of filling then top with another medallion, a second layer of filling and a third chicken slice. Wrap the phyllo round the chicken. Place seam side down in an oiled baking dish. Repeat to make six rolls. Brush with the remaining tablespoon of oil.

Bake for 45 minutes till brown. Warm the sauce and serve with the rolls.

Chicken with Peanuts and Ginger Sauce

Serves 6

Working time: about 20 minutes

Total time: about 2 hours and 20 minutes

Calories
260
Protein
30g
Cholesterol
70mg
Total fat
12g
Saturated fat
3g
Sodium
200mg

750 g	chicken breast meat, cut into 1 cm (½ inch) cubes	**1½ lb**
12.5 cl	dry white wine	**4 fl oz**
45 g	fresh ginger, finely chopped	**1½ oz**
1	garlic clove, crushed	**1**
¼ tsp	salt	**¼ tsp**
	freshly ground black pepper	

¼ litre	unsalted chicken stock	**8 fl oz**
2 tbsp	peanut butter.	**2 tbsp**
1 tsp	tomato paste (optional)	**1 tsp**
2	spring onions, julienned	**2**
45 g	peanuts, crushed with a rolling pin	**1½ oz**
1 tbsp	safflower oil	**1 tbsp**

Make a marinade of the wine, ginger, garlic, salt and pepper, and let the chicken stand in it for 2 hours.

Near the end of the marinating time, prepare the sauce. Pour the stock into a small saucepan and whisk in the peanut butter and the tomato paste, if used. Add the spring onions and simmer the sauce over low heat, uncovered, for 2 minutes. Remove the saucepan from the heat and set it aside.

Remove the cubes from the marinade and set them aside. Strain the marinade and add it to the sauce. Return the mixture to a simmer and cook over low heat, stirring occasionally, until the sauce is thick enough to coat the back of a spoon – about 4 minutes. Remove the pan from the heat.

Roll the chicken cubes in the crushed peanuts, sparsely coating the cubes. Heat the oil in a heavy frying pan over high heat. When the oil is hot but not smoking, add the chicken cubes and lightly brown them, stirring gently to keep intact as much of the peanut coating as possible – about 3 minutes. Remove the frying pan from the heat and allow the chicken to finish cooking as it rests in the hot pan – about 2 minutes more. Transfer the chicken to a warmed platter and pour the sauce over it just before serving.

Suggested accompaniments: steamed rice; fried bananas; cucumber salad.

Yogurt-Baked Chicken with Pimientos and Chives

Serves 4

Working time: about 20 minutes

Total time: about 2 hours and 30 minutes

Calories 320

Protein 45g

Cholesterol 130mg

Total fat 11g

Saturated fat 4g

Sodium 320mg

.5 kg	chicken, quartered, skinned and fat removed	3 lb
litre	plain low-fat yogurt	8 fl oz
tbsp	finely cut fresh chives	2 tbsp
tsp	salt	¼ tsp
¼ tsp	white pepper	¼ tsp
1 tbsp	plain flour	1 tbsp
35 cl	unsalted chicken stock	12 fl oz
1 tbsp	very finely chopped pimiento	1 tbsp

To prepare the marinade, combine the yogurt, chives, salt and pepper in a shallow dish. Add the chicken and marinate it in the refrigerator for at least 2 hours.

Preheat the oven to 170°C (325°F or Mark 3). Transfer the chicken to a baking dish and reserve the marinade. Bake the chicken until the juices run clear when a thigh is pierced with the tip of a sharp knife – 25 to 30 minutes.

While the chicken is cooking, put the stock in a saucepan and bring it to the boil. Reduce the heat to maintain a slow simmer. Thoroughly mix the flour into the reserved marinade. Stir a few tablespoons of the hot stock into the marinade, then add the marinade to the stock, and simmer for 3 minutes. Add the pimiento and stir the sauce well.

Transfer the chicken from the baking dish to individual serving plates, and spoon the sauce over the pieces just before serving.

Suggested accompaniments: broad beans; cornbread.

Crêpes Filled with Chicken and Sweetcorn

Serves 4

Working time: about 30 minutes

Total time: about 1 hour

Calories **385**
Protein **26g**
Cholesterol **120mg**
Total fat **17g**
Saturated fat **5g**
Sodium **415mg**

250 g	1 cm (½ inch) cubes, chicken breast	**8 oz**
¼ tsp	salt	**¼ tsp**
	freshly ground black pepper	
½ tsp	safflower oil	**½ tsp**
	Crêpe Batter	
¼ litre	semi-skimmed milk	**8 fl oz**
1	egg yolk (reserve white for filling)	**1**
90 g	plain flour	**3 oz**
15 g	unsalted butter, melted	**½ oz**
½ tsp	turmeric	**½ tsp**
⅛ tsp	salt	**⅛ tsp**
	freshly ground black pepper	
1 tsp	fresh thyme or ¼ tsp dried thyme	**1 tsp**

½ tsp	chopped parsley	**½ tsp**
½ tsp	chopped fresh tarragon	**½ tsp**
½ tsp	chopped fresh mint	**½ tsp**
½ tsp	safflower oil for the crêpe pan	**½ tsp**
	Sweetcorn Filling and Sauce	
2 tbsp	safflower oil	**2 tbsp**
1	shallot, chopped	
165 g	uncooked sweetcorn kernels	**5½ oz**
¼ litre	unsalted chicken stock	**8 fl oz**
1 tbsp	double cream	**1 tbsp**
125 g	low-fat cottage cheese	**4 oz**
2 tbsp	finely cut fresh chives	**2 tbsp**
1	egg white	

Whisk the milk and the egg yolk in a bowl. Add flour gradually, whisking to blend. Stir in butter, turmeric, salt, pepper and herbs.

Heat a frying pan over medium-high. Pour in ½ tsp of oil and wipe with a paper towel. Swirl 2 to 3 tbsp of the batter in the pan to coat the bottom. Pour any excess back into the bowl. Cook until brown – about 30 secs – lift and turn over. Brown second side – about 15 secs. Slide the crêpe on to a plate. Repeat to make at least 8 crêpes; set aside. Preheat oven to 170°C (325°F or Mark 3).

Season the chicken and sauté for 4 mins with tbsp oil. Transfer to a bowl. Add remaining and sauté shallot for 30 secs. Add sweetcorn and sauté for mins. Remove ⅓ of the sweetcorn and add it to the chicken. Add the stock and cream to the pan simmer for 3 mins then purée the mixture to make a sauce. Add cottage cheese, 1 tbsp chives and egg white to chicken and sweetcorn; mix well. Roll each crêpe round 4 tbsp of this mixture. Place crêpes in oiled baking dish, cover with sauce, and bake for 20 mins. Serve garnished with chives.

Peach-Glazed Poussins with Ginger

Serves 4

Working time: about 0 minutes

Total time: about 0 minutes

Calories 330

Protein 23g

Cholesterol 45mg

Total fat 11g

Saturated fat 2g

Sodium 490mg

Two	poussins, halved, backbones removed	Two	2 tbsp	grated fresh ginger root	2 tbsp
0 g		1½ lb	1 tbsp	safflower oil	1 tbsp
.5 cl	orange juice	6 fl oz	1	spring onion, finely sliced	1
5 g	dried peaches, thinly sliced	4 oz	2 tbsp	brown sugar	2 tbsp
tbsp	low-sodium soy sauce, or naturally fermented shoyu	1 tbsp	1 tbsp	fresh lime juice	1 tbsp
			½ tsp	salt	½ tsp

eheat the grill. To make the glaze, combine e orange juice, peaches, ginger, soy sauce, fflower oil, spring onion, brown sugar and ne juice in a small saucepan over medium at. Cook, stirring once, for 5 minutes. Set the aze aside.

Preheat the oven to 190°C (375°F or Mark 5). rinkle the poussins with the salt and put them in side up on a grill pan. To render some of

their fat, place the birds under the grill, close to the heat, and grill them until light brown – 3 to 5 minutes. Remove the birds from the grill pan to an ovenproof casserole. Coat the poussins with the peach glaze and bake them for 25 minutes.

Suggested accompaniment: green beans with toasted almonds.

Oven-Fried Cinnamon Chicken

Serves 4

Working
time: about
15 minutes

Total time:
about
1 hour

Calories
425
Protein
47g
Cholestero
125mg
Total fat
17g
Saturated fa
3g
Sodium
565mg

1.5 kg	chicken, quartered and skinned	**3 lb**
½ tsp	salt	**½ tsp**
½ tsp	freshly ground white pepper	**½ tsp**
4 tbsp	plain flour	**4 tbsp**
¼ tsp	turmeric	**¼ tsp**

1 tsp	cinnamon	**1 ts**
3	egg whites	
60 g	fresh breadcrumbs	**2**
2 tbsp	safflower oil	**2 tbs**

Preheat the oven to 170°C (325°F or Mark 3). Mix the salt, pepper and flour, and spread on a plate. In a small bowl, whisk the turmeric and cinnamon into the egg whites. Dredge the chicken pieces in the flour, then dip them in the egg whites and coat them with the breadcrumbs.

In a fireproof pan or shallow casserole large enough to hold the chicken pieces in a single layer, heat the oil over medium heat. Lay the pieces bone side up in the pan and brown them lightly on one side – about 2 minutes. Turn the

pieces over, put the pan in the oven, and bak for 30 minutes.

Remove the pan and increase the ove temperature to 230°C (450°F or Mark 8). Wa about 5 minutes, then return to the oven and l the coating crisp for 4 or 5 minutes, taking car not to burn it.

Suggested accompaniment: sautéed cherr tomatoes.

Chicken Breasts with Courgettes in Red Wine Sauce

Serves 6

Working time: about 35 minutes

Total time: about 50 minutes

Calories 385

Protein 29g

Cholesterol 85mg

Total fat 16g

Saturated fat 5g

Sodium 250mg

4	chicken breasts, skinned and boned (500 g/1 lb)	4
¼ tsp	salt	¼ tsp
½ tsp	freshly ground black pepper	½ tsp
2	courgettes, sliced into 1 cm (½ inch) rounds	2
2 tbsp	safflower oil	2 tbsp
1	garlic clove, finely chopped	1
35 cl	unsalted chicken stock	12 fl oz
1 tbsp	finely chopped shallots	1 tbsp
90 g	onions, finely chopped	3 oz
30 g	celery, finely chopped	1 oz
30 g	carrots, finely chopped	1 oz
½ litre	red wine	16 fl oz
1 tbsp	double cream	1 tbsp
½ tsp	finely chopped fresh sage, or ¼ tsp dried sage	½ tsp
15 g	unsalted butter	½ oz

Sprinkle the chicken breasts with half of the salt and ¼ teaspoon of the pepper. Sprinkle the courgettes with the remaining salt and pepper. Heat 1 tablespoon of the oil in a heavy frying pan over medium-high heat. Lightly brown the breasts in the pan – about 2 minutes on each side. Remove the breasts and sauté the courgettes and garlic for about 1 minute in the oil remaining in the pan. Remove the courgettes and deglaze the pan with 12.5 cl (4 fl oz) of the stock. Reduce the heat to low and return the breasts to the pan. Simmer, partly covered, until the meat feels firm but springy to the touch – 10 to 12 minutes.

While the breasts are cooking, prepare the sauce. Heat the remaining tablespoon of oil over medium-low heat in a heavy-bottomed saucepan. Add the shallots, onions, celery and carrots, and cook until the onions are translucent – about 10 minutes. Pour in the wine, increase the heat to medium, and cook until reduced by half – about 7 minutes. Add the cream, sage and the remaining stock. Again reduce by half. Purée the sauce in a food processor or blender and strain it. When the chicken breasts are done, move them to the side of the pan and pour in the sauce. Stir the sauce to mix it thoroughly, then whisk in the butter. Return the courgettes to the pan to heat through, and serve.

Lime and Mint Chicken

Serves 6

Working time: about 15 minutes

Total time: about 4 hours and 15 minutes

Calories 250

Protein 27g

Cholesterol 100mg

Total fat 12g

Saturated fat 3g

Sodium 185mg

12	chicken thighs, skinned	**12**
½ tsp	sugar	**½ tsp**
	Lime Marinade	
¼ litre	fresh lime juice	**8 fl oz**
8 cl	dry white wine	**3 fl oz**
45 g	fresh mint leaves, chopped, plus 6 whole mint sprigs reserved for	**1½ oz**
1½ tsp	cumin seeds, crushed, or ¾ tsp ground cumin	**1½ tsp**
3	spring onions, thinly sliced	**3**
1	large dried red chili pepper, seeded and thinly sliced, or ½ to ¾ tsp crushed red pepper flakes	**1**
¼ tsp	salt	**¼ tsp**

Combine the marinade ingredients in a shallow bowl or dish large enough to hold the chicken thighs. Put the thighs in the bowl and coat them with the marinade. Cover the bowl and refrigerate it for 4 to 6 hours.

Preheat the grill. Remove the chicken from the marinade and arrange the pieces in a grill pan. Strain the marinade into a small bowl and reserve both the strained liquid and the drained mint mixture. Grill the chicken 10 to 15 cm (4 to 6 inches) below the heat source until it is browned – 6 to 8 minutes. Remove the pan from the grill and turn the pieces over. Spoon some

of the mint mixture over each thigh. Grill the thighs until the juices run clear when a piece is pierced with the tip of a sharp knife – 6 to 8 minutes more.

Meanwhile, stir the sugar into the strained marinade. Put the liquid in a small pan and boil it over high heat for 2 minutes, stirring frequently, to produce a light sauce.

To serve, spoon some of the sauce over each thigh and garnish with the mint sprigs.

Suggested accompaniments: baked sweet potatoes; steamed cauliflower.

Grilled Chicken with Malt Vinegar and Basil

Serves 4

Working time: about 30 minutes

Total time: about 1 day

Calories 280

Protein 30g

Cholesterol 105mg

Total fat 15g

Saturated fat 4g

Sodium 235mg

4	whole chicken legs, skinned	4
17.5 cl	malt vinegar	6 fl oz
12.5 cl	dry white wine	4 fl oz
2	large shallots, thinly sliced	2
2 tsp	ground mace	2 tsp
	freshly ground black pepper	
2 tbsp	chopped fresh basil leaves, or 2 tsp dried basil	2 tbsp
¼ tsp	salt	¼ tsp

To prepare the marinade, combine the vinegar, wine, shallots, mace, pepper and basil in a saucepan. Bring the mixture to a simmer over medium heat and cook for 2 minutes. Sprinkle the chicken legs with the salt and set them in a shallow baking dish. Pour the marinade over the chicken and cover the dish with plastic film. Refrigerate for 8 hours or overnight.

Preheat the grill. Remove the legs from the marinade and arrange them on a foil-lined grill pan. Reserve the marinade. Grill the legs 8 to 10 cm (3½ to 4 inches) below the heat source for about 8 minutes on each side, brushing them with the marinade every 4 minutes. The chicken is done when the juices run clear from a thigh pierced with the tip of a sharp knife.

Suggested accompaniments: boiled new potatoes; steamed red cabbage.

Chicken Breasts with Radishes

Serves 4

Working time: about 30 minutes

Total time: about 1 day

Calories 215

Protein 27g

Cholesterol 70mg

Total fat 4g

Saturated fat 2g

Sodium 200mg

4	chicken breasts, skinned and boned, wings severed at the second joint from the tip	4
¼ tsp	salt	¼ tsp
6	large radishes, thinly sliced	6
¼ litre	red wine vinegar	8 fl oz
12.5 cl	dry white wine	4 fl oz
1½ tbsp	chopped fresh tarragon leaves, or ½ tbsp dried tarragon	1½ tbsp
	freshly ground black pepper	
2 tbsp	honey	2 tbsp

Sprinkle both sides of the breasts with the salt. With the knife held perpendicular to the long edge of a breast, cut diagonally into the smooth side of the flesh to make four 1 cm (½ inch) deep slits at 2 cm (¾ inch) intervals across the breast. Cut similar diagonal slits in the other breasts. Cover the bottom of a shallow dish with radishes and lay breasts, cut side down, on top.

To prepare the marinade, combine the vinegar, wine, tarragon, pepper and honey in a saucepan. Bring to a simmer over medium heat, and cook for 2 minutes. Stir the marinade and pour it over the breasts. Cover the dish with plastic film and refrigerate for 8 hours or overnight.

Preheat the grill when you are ready to cook the chicken. Arrange cut side down in a foil-lined grill pan. Reserve the marinade for basting.

Grill the chicken 8 to 10 cm (3½ to 4 inches) below the heat source for 4 minutes on the first side, basting once. Turn and grill them on the second side for 2 minutes. Remove the breasts from the grill and tuck one, two or three radish slices into each of the slits, forming a fish scale pattern. Grill the chicken for another 2 minutes. Make a small cut in the thick portion of a breast to see if the meat has turned white. If it is still pink, grill it for 1 or 2 minutes more.

Pour the accumulated cooking juices over the chicken breasts and serve.

Suggested accompaniment: watercress and red onion salad.

Chicken Thighs Grilled with Sherry and Honey

Serves 4

Working (and total) time: about 25 minutes

Calories 340

Protein 28g

Cholesterol 100mg

Total fat 11g

Saturated fat 3g

Sodium 385mg

	chicken thighs, skinned	**8**	**1 tbsp**	low-sodium soy sauce, or naturally fermented shoyu	**1 tbsp**
litre	dry sherry	**8 fl oz**	**1 tbsp**	cornflour, mixed with 2 tbsp dry sherry	**1 tbsp**
tbsp	honey	**3 tbsp**			
	garlic cloves, finely chopped	**4**	**¼ tsp**	salt	**¼ tsp**
tbsp	red wine vinegar	**3 tbsp**			

Boil the sherry in a small saucepan until it is reduced by half – about 7 minutes. Remove the pan from the stove and whisk in the honey, garlic, vinegar and soy sauce. Return the pan to the heat and whisk the cornflour mixture into the sauce. Bring the sauce to the boil and cook for 1 minute, whisking constantly. Remove the pan from the heat and let the sauce cool.

Preheat the grill. Sprinkle the salt on both sides of the thighs and lay them bone side up on a rack in a roasting pan. Brush liberally with the sauce, then grill them 10 to 15 cm (4 to 6 inches) from the heat source for 6 to 7 minutes. Turn over and brush again with sauce. Grill for 3 or 4 minutes more, then brush again with the remaining sauce. Continue grilling until the juices run clear when a thigh is pierced with the tip of a sharp knife – 5 to 7 minutes more. Transfer the thighs to a platter and trickle any remaining sauce from the roasting pan over them.

Suggested acompaniment: mange-tout sautéed with water chestnuts and soy sauce.

Dry Martini Poussins

Serves 4

Working time: about 30 minutes

Total time: 1 to 2 days

Calories 300

Protein 28g

Cholesterol 90mg

Total fat 14g

Saturated fat 4g

Sodium 360mg

Four **500 g**	poussins, giblets reserved for another use, cavities washed and patted dry	**Four** **1 lb**
2 tbsp **2**	juniper berries, crushed lemons, rind only, cut into 5 mm (¼ inch) strips	**2 tbsp** **2**
½ litre **17.5 cl** **4 tbsp** **½ tsp**	unsalted chicken stock gin dry vermouth salt freshly ground black pepper	**16 fl oz** **6 fl oz** **4 tbsp** **½ tsp**

To make the marinade, combine the juniper berries, lemon rind, 35 cl (12 fl oz) of the stock, two thirds of the gin, vermouth, salt and pepper in a bowl. Place the birds in a deep dish that holds them snugly, and pour the marinade over. Swirl some of the marinade into the cavity of each bird. Cover the dish with a lid or plastic film, and refrigerate for 24 to 48 hours. Turn the birds from time to time as they marinate.

Preheat the oven to 190°C (375°F or Mark 5). Remove the birds from the marinade and put 1 tablespoon of the marinade liquid, a few of the crushed juniper berries and some of the lemon rind in the cavity of each bird. Discard the remaining marinade. Tie each pair of legs together with string. Arrange birds breast side up on the rack of a roasting pan so that they do not touch. Roast until golden-brown – 40 to 50 minutes. Pour the juices, juniper berries and lemon rind from the cavity of each poussin into the pan, and set the birds on a warmed platter.

To the sauce, remove the rack and place the roasting pan over medium-high heat. Add the remaining stock and gin. Cook the sauce, stirring with a wooden spoon to dislodge any brown bits, until the liquid is reduced by about half and has thickened – 7 to 10 minutes. Strain the sauce and serve it with the birds. Garnish, if you like, with twists of fresh lemon peel.

Suggested accompaniments: steamed baby carrots; new potatoes.

Thyme-Roasted Chicken

Serves 4

Working time: about 30 minutes

Total time: about 1 hour and 30 minutes

Calories 295

Protein 38g

Cholesterol 80mg

Total fat 12g

Saturated fat 4g

Sodium 380mg

1.75 to 2 kg	chicken, giblets reserved for another use, rinsed and patted dry	3½ to 4 lb	6–8	bay leaves, crumbled into small bits	6–8
½ tsp	salt	½ tsp	12.5 cl	dry white wine	4 fl oz
	freshly ground black pepper				
1 tbsp	fresh thyme leaves, stems reserved for flavouring the cavity	1 tbsp			

Season the body cavity with ¼ tsp of the salt and some pepper. Working from the edge of the cavity, gently lift the skin covering the breast, taking care not to tear it, and distribute the thyme leaves under the skin so that they evenly cover the meat. Let the skin fall back into place. Place the thyme stems and the bay leaves in the cavity. Prepare chicken for roasting by trussing it. Preheat the oven to 200°C (400°F or Mark 6).

Select a stockpot that has a tight-fitting lid and is large enough to accommodate the chicken. Fill the pot 2.5 cm (1 inch) deep with water. Place the chicken in the pot on a rack high enough to hold the bird clear of the water. Set the pot over high heat, cover tightly, and steam the chicken for 15 minutes to begin to render its fat.

Carefully remove the bird from the pot and transfer it to the rack of a roasting pan. Season the outside of the bird with the remaining salt and some pepper. Roast the chicken until it is a light golden-brown all over – 40 to 45 minutes.

Remove the chicken and pour the contents of its cavity into the roasting pan. Add the white wine and ¼ litre (8 fl oz) of water. Place the pan over medium heat and simmer, scraping up any deposits, until reduced by half – 7 to 10 minutes.

Carve the chicken and arrange the meat on a warmed platter. Strain the reduced sauce, and spoon it over the chicken.

Suggested accompaniment: julienned carrots steamed with currants.

Roast Chicken with Apples, Turnips and Garlic

Serves 4

Working time: about 30 minutes

Total time: about 1 hour and 30 minutes

Calories 380

Protein 39g

Cholesterol 105mg

Total fat 17g

Saturated fat 5g

Sodium 195mg

1.5 kg	chicken	**3 lb**	**2 – 3**	Golden Delicious apples, peeled,	**2 – 3**
1 tbsp	paprika	**1 tbsp**		cored and cut into eighths	
½ tsp	freshly ground black pepper	**½ tsp**	**6**	garlic cloves, peeled	**6**
⅛ tsp	salt	**⅛ tsp**		juice of half a lemon	
5 g	unsalted butter	**⅙ oz**			
3	small turnips, peeled, quartered and thinly sliced	**3**			

Preheat the oven to 170°C (325°F or Mark 3). Mix the paprika, pepper and salt and rub the chicken inside and out with them.

Butter a roasting pan and put the chicken in it. Arrange the apples, turnips and garlic around the bird. Trickle the lemon juice over the top of the apples and turnips. Roast the chicken until it is golden-brown all over and a leg moves easily when it is wiggled up and down – 65 to 75 minutes. Baste the bird with the pan juices two or three times during the cooking.

When the chicken is done, skim the fat from the pan and mash the apples, turnips and garlic together with the pan juices. Serve in a seperate bowl.

Suggested accompaniment: mange-tout or sugarsnap peas.

Cold Chicken and Asparagus with Lemon-Tarragon

Serves 4

Working
(and total)
Time: about
45 minutes

Calories
280

Protein
29g

Cholesterol
70mg

Total fat
15g

Saturated fat
2g

Sodium
135mg

	chicken breasts, skinned and boned (about 500 g/1 lb)	4	1 tbsp	chopped shallot, or 2 spring onions, finely chopped	1 tbsp
0	asparagus spears, ends trimmed, peeled ⅓ of the way up the stalks	20	½ tsp	fresh thyme, or ⅛ tsp dried thyme	½ tsp
tsp	safflower oil	½ tsp	1½ tsp	chopped fresh tarragon, or ½ tsp dried tarragon	1½ tsp
tsp	salt	⅛ tsp	2 tbsp	safflower oil	2 tbsp
	freshly ground black pepper		1 tbsp	virgin olive oil	1 tbsp
	sweet red pepper, julienned	½	1	garlic clove, chopped	1
			1 tbsp	chopped parsley	1 tbsp
	Lemon-Tarragon Vinaigrette		1 tsp	sugar	1 tsp
tbsp	fresh lemon juice	3 tbsp		freshly ground black pepper	

To make the vinaigrette, combine the shallot, lemon juice, thyme and tarragon. Stand for 10 minutes, whisk in the oils, the garlic, parsley, sugar and pepper. Stand for 10 minutes more.

In a heavy frying pan, heat the safflower oil over very low heat. Sprinkle the breasts with the salt and pepper. Place the breasts in the pan and cover them with a heavy plate to weight them down and preserve their juices. Cook the breasts on one side for 5 minutes, turn, and cook for another 3 to 4 minutes. The meat should feel firm but springy to the touch, and there should

be no visible pink along the edges. Remove from the pan and cool in the refrigerator for at least 10 minutes or until ready to serve.

To cook the asparagus, place in a pan with a tight-fitting lid, together with 4 tablespoons of water. Cover, boil, and cook until tender but still crisp – about 2 minutes. Drain, rinse under cold running water, chill, and keep cool.

Slice the breasts on the diagonal and arrange each one on serving plates with five asparagus spears. Garnish with the red pepper and spoon the vinaigrette over the chicken and asparagus.

Spatchcocked Chicken with Basil-Yogurt Sauce

Serves 4

Working time: about 25 minutes

Total time: about 1 hour and 15 minutes

Calories 390

Protein 45g

Cholesterol 90mg

Total fat 20g

Saturated fat 6g

Sodium 365mg

1.5 kg	chicken, rinsed and patted dry	**3 lb**	**2**	garlic cloves, finely chopped	
¼ litre	plain low-fat yogurt	**8 fl oz**	**1 tbsp**	virgin olive oil	**1 tbs**
60 g	fresh basil leaves, chopped, or spinach leaves, lightly steamed and squeezed dry	**2 oz**	**5 tbsp**	freshly grated Parmesan or Romano cheese	**5 tbs**
3	spring onions, chopped	**3**	**⅛ tsp**	salt	**⅛ ts**
				freshly ground black pepper	

Prepare the bird for roasting. Preheat the oven to 200°C (400°F or Mark 6). Cover the bottom of a large pot with 2.5 cm (½ inch) water. Set a steamer or rack in the pot, and bring the water to the boil. Place the chicken skin side up on the steamer. Cover tightly and steam the chicken for 15 minutes over high heat.

While the chicken is steaming, make the sauce. Combine the yogurt, basil or spinach, spring onions, garlic, oil and half the Parmesan cheese in a food processor or blender. Process until smooth, then transfer the sauce to a sauceboat and set it aside at room temperature.

Set the chicken on a rack in a roasting pan. Sprinkle with salt and some pepper. Roast until skin is crispy, light brown – about 25 minutes

Remove the bird from the oven and sprinkl the remaining cheese over it. Return the chicke to the oven and roast until the cheese is golden brown – 8 to 10 minutes more.

Allow the chicken to stand 10 minutes, carv into serving pieces. Pass the sauce separately

Suggested accompaniments: stewed tomatoes brown rice.

Editor's Note: The process of steaming followe by roasting helps to defat the chicken, resulting in a crisp skin and fewer calories.

Chilled Chicken Couscous with Lime

Serves 4

Working time: about 30 minutes

Total time: about 40 minutes

Calories 435

Protein 23g

Cholesterol 55mg

Total fat 18g

Saturated fat 3g

Sodium 215mg

350 g	chicken meat, cut into 2 cm (¾ inch) pieces	12 oz
2 tbsp	finely chopped onion	2 tbsp
4 tbsp	safflower oil	4 tbsp
175 g	couscous	6 oz
¼ litre	unsalted chicken stock	8 fl oz
5 tbsp	fresh lime juice	5 tbsp
1	garlic clove, finely chopped	1
4 tsp	fresh thyme, or 1 tsp dried thyme	4 tsp
¼ tsp	salt	¼ tsp
	freshly ground black pepper	
6	spring onions, trimmed and finely chopped	6
1	sweet red pepper, seeded, deribbed and chopped into 1 cm (½ inch) squares	1
	lettuce leaves (for serving)	

In a heavy frying with a tight-fitting lid, sauté the onion in 1 tablespoon of the oil over medium-high heat for about 2 minutes. Stir in the couscous, the stock and ¼ litre (8 fl oz) of water, and boil rapidly for about 2 minutes. Remove the pan from the heat and cover it; let it stand for 5 minutes. Remove the lid, fluff up the couscous with a fork, and transfer the mixture to a large mixing bowl. Put in the refrigerator to cool.

For the dressing, combine 4 tablespoons of lime juice, garlic, thyme, salt and some pepper. Add half the spring onions and set aside.

Add another tablespoon of oil to the pan and set it over high heat. When the oil is hot, add the chicken pieces and sauté them, stirring frequently, until lightly browned – 4 to 5 minutes. Stir in the remaining tablespoon of lime juice and a generous grinding of pepper. Using a slotted spoon, transfer the pieces to a bowl. Refrigerate them for at least 10 minutes.

Whisk the remaining 2 tablespoons of oil into the dressing mixture. Remove the couscous and the chicken from the refrigerator. Stir the dressing into the couscous. Finally, add the chicken, the remaining spring onions and the red pepper, and mix well. Serve each portion on a bed of lettuce.

Useful weights and measures

Weight Equivalents

Avoirdupois		Metric
1 ounce	=	28.35 grams
1 pound	=	254.6 grams
2.3 pounds	=	1 kilogram

Liquid Measurements

$^1/_4$ pint	=	$1^1/_2$ decilitres
$^1/_2$ pint	=	$^1/_4$ litre
scant 1 pint	=	$^1/_2$ litre
$1^3/_4$ pints	=	1 litre
1 gallon	=	4.5 litres

Liquid Measures

1 pint	= 20 fl oz	= 32 tablespoons
$^1/_2$ pint	= 10 fl oz	= 16 tablespoons
$^1/_4$ pint	= 5 fl oz	= 8 tablespoons
$^1/_8$ pint	= $2^1/_2$ fl oz	= 4 tablespoons
$^1/_{16}$ pint	= $1^1/_4$ fl oz	= 2 tablespoons

Solid Measures

1 oz almonds, ground = $3^3/_4$ level tablespoons

1 oz breadcrumbs fresh = 7 level tablespoons

1 oz butter, lard = 2 level tablespoons

1 oz cheese, grated = $3^1/_2$ level tablespoons

1 oz cocoa = $2^3/_4$ level tablespoons

1 oz desiccated coconut = $4^1/_2$ tablespoons

1 oz cornflour = $2^1/_2$ tablespoons

1 oz custard powder = $2^1/_2$ tablespoons

1 oz curry powder and spices = 5 tablespoons

1 oz flour = 2 level tablespoons

1 oz rice, uncooked = $1^1/_2$ tablespoons

1 oz sugar, caster and granulated = 2 tablespoons

1 oz icing sugar = $2^1/_2$ tablespoons

1 oz yeast, granulated = 1 level tablespoon

American Measures

16 fl oz	=1 American pint
8 fl oz	=1 American standard cup
0.50 fl oz	=1 American tablespoon

(*slightly smaller than British Standards Institute tablespoon*)

0.16 fl oz	=1 American teaspoon

Australian Cup Measures

(*Using the 8-liquid-ounce cup measure*)

1 cup flour	4 oz
1 cup sugar (crystal or caster)	8 oz
1 cup icing sugar (free from lumps)	5 oz
1 cup shortening (butter, margarine)	8 oz
1 cup brown sugar (lightly packed)	4 oz
1 cup soft breadcrumbs	2 oz
1 cup dry breadcrumbs	3 oz
1 cup rice (uncooked)	6 oz
1 cup rice (cooked)	5 oz
1 cup mixed fruit	4 oz
1 cup grated cheese	4 oz
1 cup nuts (chopped)	4 oz
1 cup coconut	$2^1/_2$ oz

Australian Spoon Measures

	level tablespoon
1 oz flour	2
1 oz sugar	$1^1/_2$
1 oz icing sugar	2
1 oz shortening	1
1 oz honey	1
1 oz gelatine	2
1 oz cocoa	3
1 oz cornflour	$2^1/_2$
1 oz custard powder	$2^1/_2$

Australian Liquid Measures

(*Using 8-liquid-ounce cup*)

1 cup liquid	8 oz
$2^1/_2$ cups liquid	20 oz (1 pint)
2 tablespoons liquid	1 oz
1 gill liquid	5 oz ($^1/_4$ pint)